The Faith to Continue On...

WALKING WITH THE LORD DURING DIFFICULT TIMES

ELLIS D. JIMMERSON

WESTBOW
PRESS®
A DIVISION OF THOMAS NELSON
& ZONDERVAN

WestBow Press books may be ordered through booksellers or by contacting:

WestBow Press
A Division of Thomas Nelson & Zondervan
1663 Liberty Drive
Bloomington, IN 47403
www.westbowpress.com
844-714-3454

Scripture quotations marked KJV are taken from the King James Version.

Scripture quotations marked NKJV are taken from the New King James Version®. Copyright © 1982 by Thomas Nelson. Used by permission. All rights reserved.

Scripture quotations marked AMP are taken from the Amplified® Bible, Copyright © 2015 by The Lockman Foundation. Used by permission.

Scripture quotations marked MSG are taken from The Message. Copyright © 1993, 1994, 1995, 1996, 2000, 2001, 2002. Used by permission of NavPress Publishing Group.

ISBN: 978-1-6642-5563-0 (sc)
ISBN: 978-1-6642-5562-3 (e)

Print information available on the last page.

WestBow Press rev. date: 02/04/2022

Dedicated to my Mom & Dad,
'Neshia & Amani

INTRODUCTION

As we began to journey through this book it is imperative that I start this journey with you by saying that this book should not be viewed as devotional. This isn't made to be a book that keeps you reading for the sake of just having your personal devotion time. Though having devotional time with God is a great thing, this book is geared toward helping the reader learn how to trust in God's word, God's process and God's view. With the gospel of Jesus Christ according to Mark chapter 5 we begin examining the brief narrative of the synagogue ruler named Jairus. As we look into the narrative of Jairus there are a couple of entities we must pay close attention to: 1) His power, prestige & position 2) his posture toward the Prince of Peace 3) his pleading for what's connected to him 4) his patience and placement during the miracle of someone else 5) his atmosphere and attitude concerning his predicament and 6) the process needed to receive the help he longed for. Seeking God for a miracle is nothing new to the Christian believer and neither is wondering when we will ever get that miracle. Looking to God to help us where we are brings about so much more in us during the process than the actual outcome of the miracle. Even though we're excited about the outcome, we should also pay close attention to what God is doing in us, with us, through us and around us as we journey to the final outcome. It's moments like this that we miss God because we're so honed into receiving our miracle that we fail to value the process of getting there. Our attitudes, mindsets and even our atmospheres will be affected as we journey to the end result of the blessing that lies ahead. We live in a microwave society where we want what we want when we want it and most of the time, we want what we want NOW!!! We don't care about the process of getting what we want because we're so set on what we have to do and what we have been doing and because of what we went through and what we have to do, that entitles us to get what we want right away. As often as I've been in a restaurant to get a delicious steak cooked well done, I must admit to myself that I get a little impatient when my steak takes time to cook. I see a lot of people in the same restaurant come in after me getting their food before I get mine and I get mad, impatient and even a little bit uptight because no one should get their food before me if I got here first. What I had to realize was that because of the item that I'd ordered and the way I wanted it served, it took time to prepare if I wanted a quality – served product. As we go through this faith manual, we are going to learn together that the quality of what we desire from God comes with a process. In this process we will experience the breakdown and breakthrough of others, the shifting focus from one who has prestige into one who's looking for help and how to maintain faith in God in the face of limited thinking people.

With that being said: are you ready to strive for the quality of God? Are you ready to operate in the gift of patience? Do you want to learn how to trust God in the midst of disagreeable atmospheres? Are you willing to eliminate the variables that can keep you from reaching the final outcome you long to witness? If you've said yes to all of these questions, then let the journey begin.

WHEN THE POWERFUL & POSITIONED
SEEK THE PRINCE OF PEACE

And behold, one of the rulers of the synagogue came, Jairus by name.
Mark 5:22a KJV

Before we get to our friend, Jairus, let's do a quick review. In Mark chapter 1 we find Jesus being baptized by John the Baptist at the Jordan River. After being baptized by John the Baptist, we hear the voice of God burst out of heaven and the Holy Spirit descending like a dove as God speaks of His approval of His Son and calls Him His "beloved Son." Jesus is led by the Spirit to be tempted by the devil in the wilderness for forty days. After Jesus' dealing with Satan, He progresses to Galilee preaching the gospel of the kingdom of God telling people everywhere to repent and believe the gospel. Jesus begins collecting His team of disciples, along with casting out unclean spirits out of a man in the temple synagogue while teaching and continues healing the sick and diseased in Capernaum, including the mother-in-law of Simon (1:30-31). Jesus continues to preach the gospel throughout all of Galilee and there came to Him a leper pleading and kneeling down to Jesus to cleanse him of his leprosy. After Jesus is moved with compassion on the leper, He puts forth His hands, touches the leper and tells the leper be clean. As Jesus speaks on the leper's cleansing, immediately the leper is cleansed and Jesus charges him not to tell no man except the priest to be certain of the man's cleansing of leprosy according to the law of Moses. Instead, the man chose to spread the good news of his healing (1:40-45). After verse 45 Jesus' name is now spreading abroad due to his powerful teaching and his display of miracle working power.

Jesus has made a huge impact on the scene for those who were looking for healing and breakthrough. But, for others, Jesus is performing acts of miracles that the religious elite could not do. Who is this man that has the people talking? Why are these people flocking behind Him instead of seeking the religious leaders for their help? Jesus is reaching out to a world of people who long to see a change. They're used to being told "thou shall not." They're used to being told "you can't do that" or "we caught you doing that." Maybe the people were looking for someone to finally say "here's what you do." As Jesus is making His way through this book, He's also building up his team of disciples. He's recruiting pupils to learn how to operate from a kingdom perspective. He's training a group of individuals who will have His heart and passion for transforming the lives of those who have been downtrodden and in despair.

Religious leaders of Jesus' day are hearing about the fame of Jesus and they're even trying to find ways to corner Jesus and the teachings He has shared with the people. These leaders have become slaves to the manuscript of the law of Moses, but they never seemed to grasp the heart of the law. Here's a question: if God sent His Son to redeem mankind back to Him, wouldn't God want me to have an understanding of the law He gave to keep me protected from myself? It's quite interesting how we who serve as clergy and teachers of the word of God are quick to teach from a book to condemn and convict people instead of understanding that the God of the bible is also a God who is concerned about the well-being of his creation. So much so that He gave His only begotten Son up to die for the sins of all people past, present and future. God is not a God who finds pleasure in punishing us just for the sake of punishing us. In fact, let's review how much God loves us in these following scriptures:

> *For when we were still without strength, in due time Christ died for the ungodly. For scarcely for a righteous man will one die; yet perhaps for a good man someone would even dare to die. But God demonstrates His*

own love toward us, in that while we were still sinners, Christ died for us.
~Romans 5:6-8 NKJV

For God so loved the world that He gave His only begotten Son, that whoever
believes in Him should not perish but have everlasting life. ~John 3:16 NKJV

God's love is a love that's broad enough to reach anyone, yet specific enough to overlook no one.

In looking at the first four chapters of Mark we see how Jesus has impacted the lives of what many may call "common folk." The people whose lives have been impacted by the ministry of Jesus were probably low to middle class people. Jesus has impacted the lives of demon-possessed people, physically challenged people, poor people, wayward living people, oppressed and poverty-stricken people, so on and so forth. Now, as we enter into chapter 5, after Jesus heals the man with an unclean spirit, Jesus is on the way to be encountered by a man of authority. Ladies and gentlemen, I present to some and introduce to others Jairus, the synagogue ruler.

The text doesn't give us a plethora of history concerning Jairus nor does it even tell us much about his background and pedigree. However, let's attempt to break down Jairus by what is obvious – his position. In Mark 5:22 KJV the bible describes Jairus as *one of the rulers of the synagogue.* One who held the title of ruler of the synagogue held a very important office when it came to the synagogue. When it came to the temple synagogue, the ruler of the synagogue was third in command (the high priest was first in command while the chief of the priests was second). In provincial synagogues the ruler was supreme. No one was eligible to this office until he had a certificate from the Great Sanhedrin that he possessed the requisite qualifications. The election of the ruler, however, was by the members of the synagogue. As far as the job description of the ruler, his responsibility was to supervise all matters connected to worship (Freeman, 1996, 443). What a responsibility for an individual like Jairus. When it comes to the worship activities in the synagogue, nothing was getting past Jairus. He had to approve the order of worship, oversee the activities of worship and allow or disapprove the acts of worship. Have you ever been in a place of authority where you had to be the one who approved or disapproved of what would happen next? Did you have to deal with the backlash of others based on your final decision? Many of the people who have served in positions of leadership have gotten a little bit over their heads when it comes to the power they were given to operate. At times we've gotten too consumed with the authority that we lose sight of the fact that we're servants first. There's nothing wrong with being firm in your leadership and keeping things tight with the people who work under your management, but as a leader you must make sure that even in your leadership, you display the heart of a servant. "How can I help you?"

We don't see any signs of pompous attitude from Jairus, but I must establish the fact that throughout Jesus' earthly ministry He dealt with many of arrogant, religious leaders who consistently tried to back Him into a corner hoping that Jesus would curl up and wither away to their demeaning show of pompous leadership. It's always been my philosophy that managers manage businesses, but leaders lead people. Managers can manage paperwork, establish and maintain policies, processes and procedures, but leaders can influence, empower and impact people to perform at their best or lead them to their worst. We may not know the attitude of Jairus in his leadership role as a synagogue ruler, but as we continue on this journey of faith, let's be mindful of the fact that when you have a position of influence, don't waste it on just being a dictator in telling people what to do and what not to do. Let those who you influence know that your influence is designed to show others how to be a blessing to others even in leadership. You're not in that position for the pleasure of telling people what to do. You're in that position to remind others that faithful servanthood is what placed you in that position to show others how to serve.

As we continue on this journey with Jairus, the synagogue ruler, we find him locating Jesus and falling at Jesus' feet (Mark 5:22 KJV). This is a big observation. The man who is in charge of the temple worship came to Jesus in the form of worship. It's obvious by his actions that Jairus didn't see Jesus as a regular man. His view of Jesus was one of reverence. Up to this point, we haven't seen Jairus bow down to no man in worship. Nonetheless, Jairus sees Jesus and falls at His feet. Why would Jairus, a synagogue ruler with authority, fall down at the feet of Jesus? Could Jairus be causing a scene for the sake of making himself look good in front of Jesus? Of course not. In fact, we find in Mark 5:23 KJV that Jairus besought Jesus greatly because of his dying daughter. We'll get to the daughter much later.

Jairus had a need concerning his daughter and his power and position was not even a factor. If you carefully look at the text, we are told who Jairus was. Jesus isn't told who

Jairus was. Jairus himself doesn't tell Jesus who he was or what position he held. Jairus was in a place where he needed consolation. His daughter is dying and he has no peace. We see nowhere in the text where Jairus is looking for anyone else to help him with his daughter. He saw Jesus and fell at His feet. At some point in our lives, we have to be mindful of the fact that our power, position and prestige isn't what is important to the Lord. What's important to the Lord is your longing to seek Him for what you need. For Jairus, he needed Jesus to heal his dying daughter. For many of us it may be healing from a disease or illness, deliverance from an addiction or stronghold, justice for a murdered loved one, reviving a dying ministry or maybe a financial miracle from being in debt. Whatever our need is, Jehovah Jireh has the power and ability to provide. We must not be so caught up in ourselves and our power of influence that we can't see God beyond the blindness of our own pompous and egotistical personas. There's nothing wrong with being a person of power, position and prestige, but we can't allow our level of power to block our desire for a miracle.

Let's look at an Old Testament character named Naaman as our case study concerning the powerful, positioned and prestigious. In 2nd Kings chapter 5 Naaman is the *"...commander of the army of the king of Syria,* he *was a great and honorable man in the eyes of his master, because by him the Lord had given victory to Syria. He was also a mighty man of valor, but a leper"* (5:1 NKJV). Notice all the great things we hear about Naaman: he's an army commander, a great and honorable man, by him the Lord had given victory to Syria and he was a man of valor. What a great way to be described, right? However, after all his greatness we see a comma followed by the word *but*. A comma is used to indicate the separation of elements within the grammatical structure of a sentence. The word *but* is a conjunction that precedes a negation. All of Naaman's greatness and accomplishments are separated by a fact that negates all of his power, position and prestige. All of it is separated by the fact that *he is a leper*. Naaman suffered from leprosy which was a malignant skin disease characterized by inflamed nodules under the skin as well as body parts wasting away. A female captive from Israel told the wife of Naaman that if only her master were with the prophet who is in Samaria that he would heal Naaman of his leprosy. After the king of Syria gives Naaman silver, gold and clothing for his journey he also sends a letter to the king of Israel. Once Naaman reaches the king of Israel, the king reads the letter and tears his clothes in astonishment. However, the prophet Elisha hears about the king's reading of the letter and requests that Naaman be sent to him so that he'll know that there is a prophet in Israel. Naaman, then, arrives in his majesty and grandeur with his horses and chariots while dealing with his body wasting away because of a skin disease and arrives at the door of Elisha's house. Elisha sends his servant to the door and instructs Naaman to go and wash in the Jordan River seven times and his skin will be restored and he shall be clean of his leprosy. Now, here comes the attitude of the man who has power, position and prestige. Naaman is furious and walks away wanting the prophet to come to him and heal Naaman his way (we'll focus on this point in another chapter). This great man we heard about in verse 1 can't get healed of his leprosy because of his entitlement. He came with his horses and chariots carrying silver, gold and clothing. He also has his servants riding with him to meet the prophet who sends his servant to give Naaman the plan of action to receive his healing. Then, Elisha tells the servant to tell Naaman to go wash seven times in the Jordan River, however, he views the Jordan as the worst choice of water to wash in. Naaman names all the different bodies of water that, to him, were the more pristine of rivers for him to go wash in, but because the Jordan River was not up to his "great" standards, he would refuse.

Maybe you were offered a better position at your job, but you had to train under someone you didn't like or favor too well. Maybe you were asked to serve in a ministry where you had to work with people that you wouldn't even talk to during the course of the week. Maybe you're a ministerial leader and you had to do some work in the church that, in your summation, was beneath you or wasn't your job. How can God bless you with the end result when you can't trust Him with the process? We can't allow pride, power and positions predict our progress to promotion and promise. Proverbs 11:2a says *"When pride comes, then comes shame (NKJV)."* At some point, we're going to have to learn how to turn off our pride and turn on our humility. We can't be so blinded by our prestige and influence that we forget that we have shortcomings that have the potential to show us how off we can be and have been. Whether you carry the title of Manager, Supervisor, Captain, General, President, Mayor, Pastor, Minister or the like; you are a person with vulnerabilities and errors. You're not going to get it right all the time and you don't have all the answers. As much as getting blessed is your goal, God has things along the way that would be an even greater blessing than the one you had desired to possess. You're probably saying to yourself "well I'm not in a leadership role like the ones mentioned." Well maybe you're the babysitter that the community looks to raising their children. Maybe you're the mentor of a young man finding his way in life. Maybe you're the family member who goes to church regularly and members of your family have children who don't attend, but they look to you to take the children to church with you. Where there's influence, good or bad, there's leadership. When people see you in action doing what they long to do, you're a person of power and where there is power, there is responsibility. The way you handle your influence affects them in more ways than you will ever know. People see you as an example and when you fail to utilize your influence in a positive way, you're failing them as well. Jesus says in Matthew 15:14 NKJV *"... if the blind leads the blind, both will fall into a ditch."* Do you want to be the one that's responsible for leading others in the wrong direction because you're blinded by your own influence and power?

Jairus was a man of authority who didn't bring his authority and influence to Jesus. He came to Jesus with a need that was beyond his control. He didn't send a servant of his to go and tell Jesus to come and heal his dying daughter. His name, his office and his authority weren't of any importance to himself or Jesus. He came broken and in need of a miracle. Even David, a king of Israel who defeated Goliath, a Philistine giant, came to a place in his life where a misuse of power and authority can cost you your family and your peace of mind. In 2nd Samuel chapter 11 King David stayed in his palace instead of going to war with his army. After awakening from a nap, He walks out to his balcony and sees a beautiful woman bathing named Bathsheba, the wife of Uriah the Hittite. David inquired of the woman, finds out who she is and goes forth in bringing her into his home and sleeps with her. When David receives word of Bathsheba being with child, he sends for Uriah with hopes of sending him home to be with his wife. Uriah stays in the kingdom near his men and David then tells Uriah to stay with him where they ate and drank with David to the extent that Uriah became drunk. After another failed attempt to send Uriah home, David tells his servant Joab in the form of a letter to place Uriah in the forefront of the battle where it's most fierce so that during the heat of the battle Uriah would die. After the battle David receives word that Uriah dies and moves Bathsheba into his home, marries her and she gives birth to his son and God was displeased with David. In 2nd Samuel chapter 12 the prophet Nathan was sent by God to speak with David concerning his actions. Nathan tells the story of a rich man with plenty and a poor man with one ewe lamb. A traveler came to visit the rich man and instead of slaying a lamb from his own flock, he took the poor man's only lamb and prepared it for the man who visited him. David was enraged and mentioned to Nathan that the rich man should die and repay the poor man fourfold for what he had taken. Little did David know he was referring to himself. Nathan reminds David how God was responsible for where David was in his life. All that David had was a result of God's favor upon him. Unfortunately, David's household would suffer as a result of his sin. When David found himself in a place of brokenness, he composed Psalm 51 to speak from his heart where he was and where he wanted to be in his relationship with God. His office as king was not a factor in being restored. All he desired was to be cleansed of his sin. He knew what was necessary for him to be in a reviving place with God. Look at what David says in Psalm 51:17 NKJV *"The sacrifices of God are a broken spirit, A broken and a contrite heart—These, O God, You will not despise."* He knew that God would receive him if he came to God open as a broken vessel looking to be mended back together again. No individual can perform their own surgery. They go to credible surgeons who have studied and practiced to perform specific types of surgery. This king needed a heart transplant. One that required a clean conscience and a renewed spirit. He knew who created him because he did not create himself: God did.

How often we forget that where we are in life God brought us to that place. The tangible and intangible blessings we have come by way of God being so gracious towards us and having favor upon our lives. Yet, we tend to use our power, position and prestige as a way to get what we want. We allow our influence to draw attention to ourselves and get what we want, but away from the Lord. Jesus wasn't going to move any faster or operate any differently because of who Jairus was. God knows what we stand in need of before we even come to Him, but our mindset has to come down to a place of humility when it comes to seeking God for what we stand in need of.

As we prepare to go into chapter 2, we must come to an understanding that our attitude towards God is more important than our need from God. Before we get so quick to asking, begging or pleading with God concerning what we want, we should have an attitude of gratitude and humility realizing who we are coming into the presence of. If Jairus was going to receive from the Lord concerning his daughter, his power, position and prestige would have to be thrown to the side if peace was to be obtained from the Prince of Peace.

Chapter 2

PRESENTING YOUR POSTURE BEFORE
PRESENTING YOUR PROBLEM

And behold, one of the rulers of the synagogue came, Jairus
by name. And when he saw Him, he fell at His feet…
Mark 5:22 KJV

As little children, they rarely go to their parents in the opening of a conversation and say "Hello mom and dad. How are you?" "Hey mom and dad. How was your day? Tell me all about it." Just saying that in my mind is comical because I never did that to even get what I wanted. I just simply asked if I could get it. Children are young and somewhat innocent. It's not that they're trying to be rude. It's just in their nature to ask for what they want. They're excited, anxious and impatient in their asking. They may even do things that they normally won't do to get what they want or in other words "butter us up." They know they can't do it themselves so since they can't get it themselves, they come to us – the parents.

As they matriculate as teenagers and young adults, they now want to make their own money so that the stuff they use to ask the parents for, they now want to make their own money and get it themselves. They don't want to wait for you to think about it to say either yes or no. They want what they want and they want it now. However, they fail to realize that it's a possibility that they're not ready to receive what they want. Case in point: children ages of 7-12 may want a dog. Dogs are friendly, playful and make the children go wild. On one end the child sees the fun of having a dog. On the other end the parent sees the constant, ongoing responsibility of owning a dog. Parents will tell the child about the feeding, the cleaning and the medical responsibilities of having a dog and all the child wants to know is "can I have one?" As the parent you ask the child if they are willing to feed the dog, wash the dog, clean up after the dog and walk the dog and every answer from them is yes. So, you see the happiness fill the face of the child and you finally give in and get the dog. Automatically, you see the child excited about having their dog and being playful with the dog and right away you have to remind the child of their commitment to care for the dog they said they were going to take care of. You try to be patient with the child in making sure they care for the dog, but then the child realizes that taking care of the dog is ongoing and overwhelming. Now, instead of the child taking the responsibility of caring for the dog, the shift of care now falls on the parent while the child just wants to play with the dog. It simply goes to show that the child wasn't ready for the responsibility of having the dog.

Jairus' position as ruler of the synagogue wasn't important nor was it necessary to get what he wanted from Jesus. There was no formal introduction nor was it a demand for Jairus to get what he wanted from Jesus. Jairus, ruler of the synagogue, did not make a grand entrance with an entourage following him or a representative speaking on his behalf. I'm sure that Jairus may have been wearing his synagogue attire when approaching Jesus concerning his need, but none of that mattered to Jairus. Jairus was in an open area near the seashore in Capernaum where a great multitude of people had met Jesus (Mark 5:21) and not once did Jairus care about his office, attire or his religious status in the midst of a crowd of people or Jesus. Jairus had nothing to prove to Jesus. Jesus' name had been spreading all over the place concerning His authoritative teachings and his miracle working power. Jairus was fully aware of the work of Jesus, but he also knew that what he was standing in need of he couldn't do it himself. However, he heard of the one who could – Jesus. Knowing that Jairus was in need of something that was about the life of another, someone close to him and something that he couldn't do on his own, he made haste to see Jesus concerning his plight.

At this point, Jairus did not come as an anxious, excited child who was looking for mom or dad to do something for him that he knew he couldn't do. Instead, his posture upon seeing Jesus was noticed before his request was even mentioned. We can't even get to verse

23 concerning Jairus' need because verse 22 gives us something much more important than Jairus' need – his posture before Jesus.

I remember years ago I was working as a pharmacy technician at a neighborhood grocery store. I had no intentions of working in a pharmacy because I didn't think I was knowledgeable enough, smart enough or had the education to become one. It just so happened that one of the pharmacists who worked there whom I had a great working relationship with told me that their pharmacy manager had been watching me for a long time and that he wanted to try me out as a pharmacy technician. I was humbled at the opportunity and made the necessary arrangements to come and work in the pharmacy. A few times a week I would work with the pharmacy manager on various aspects of the business such as filling prescriptions, interpreting doctors' language on dosage for prescribed medications, etc. In fact, one day he was showing me how to log in a prescription for a customer. While he was showing me how it was done, I had my arms folded. In the middle of his training me he told me that he had attended a seminar on body language and posture in business and he shared with me that one of the things that was shared in the seminar was that many of times when people fold their arms during a training or meeting at work while the facilitator was making their presentation, the arms folded was a sign of one who didn't care or was arrogant about what was taking place at the time. Immediately, I dropped my arms and kept them at my sides for the remainder of the training. I did that because I didn't want to show that I wasn't interested in what he had to share. This man had been observing me for some time now without me even knowing it and I didn't want my posture to deter me from learning how to do a great job.

What is posture? Posture is the arrangement of the body and its limbs. It presents an attitude to others by way of one's body language. Whether we know it or not our posture is being observed and it can be a deciding factor in terms of how people will approach you if they choose to do so. If your posture shows carelessness, then it's a possibility that people may refrain from approaching you. They may not even choose to have a conversation with you just because of the language your body presents. You may not mean anything by it, but it shows more than you know. There have been times I've sat in a pulpit and the preacher may say something unsound and unbiblical. I would make faces not thinking about the fact that others see me making the face. I was approached by a parishioner once about how my face was looking when the preacher was up preaching. I felt so bad because if she saw it and was kind enough to tell me about it, then there may have been others who saw it and didn't even care enough to tell me. Because of her concern I made it my business that if I heard something unsound and unbiblical from the preacher again while I was in the pulpit, I would make sure that I would catch myself before I did it again. Many times, we're not mindful of what we say and do and it will cost us. Not many people would even care enough to tell you so that you can make the proper adjustments so that it won't happen again. Since people aren't always that concerned and kind, we have to make a conscious and physical effort to make adjustments when things are uncomfortable and unsettling for us.

Jairus was in an uncomfortable, unsettling and uneasy moment in his life where his daughter was lying at the point of death. He knew that since he wasn't able to fix the problem himself, he made strides to go to the person that can. He could have approached Jesus in an arrogant fashion by sticking out his synagogue ruler chest and his religious leader nose in the air with a possible entourage speaking on his behalf, but instead of the pomp and circumstance or the arrogant approach, he comes in the presence of Jesus and before he speaks a word he falls at the feet of Jesus. Notice the position in which Jairus took: in order for Jairus to fall at Jesus' feet, he had to first be in an erected position – meaning he had to be standing. Jairus is a ruler of the synagogue who was in charge of the synagogue worship. He knew what was allowed and not allowed. He was responsible for approving or disapproving what was permissible in the worship experience. Notice where Jairus falls: he is not in the synagogue worshipping. He's not worshipping God the Father in a set place where synagogue worship is taking place. He's not worshipping in a secluded, private place. Jairus is falling at the feet of Jesus, the Son of God. He's in an open area where everyone is watching him as the ruler of the synagogue worshipping another man. Jairus has enough sense to compose himself, forget about his religious office and influence and honor the Son of God before he makes his request known to Jesus. He's desperate, but he's in order. He's uncomfortable, but he's in order. His daughter is at the point of death, but Jairus is in order. With all the emotion and circumstances that Jairus is dealing with, he's mindful to stay in order and in worship and reverence to Jesus. Jairus is not just dealing with another man. He's dealing with Immanuel (God with us).

Let's look at Luke chapter 11 for a moment. When Jesus was reaching an end to praying while in a certain place, one of His disciples inquired of Him saying "Lord, teach us to pray, as John also taught his disciples. (Luke 11:1 KJV)" There must be something to this thing called prayer. They're familiar with John the Baptist being the voice that cried out in the wilderness baptizing in the Jordan River. They've also noticed that John was a man of prayer as well as a man who was known for teaching his disciples on the essence of prayer. So, if John taught his disciples to pray, and Jesus was a man of prayer then maybe it's important for them to also become familiar with the act of prayer. Without having to think twice Jesus told them what to say. Luke 11:2 (NKJV) consisted of just divine acknowledgement. That verse solely was geared toward us just acknowledging God as to who He is (our Father), where He resides (in heaven), the reverencing of His name (Hallowed be Your name), His kingdom system welcomed (Your kingdom come), and His will be fulfilled in earth as it's already fulfilled in heaven (Your will be done on earth as it is in heaven).

When we approach God in worship, we approach Him as one who is inferior coming to The One who is superior. No matter what our social, professional or clerical status may be on earth, it's not important when we approach God. We may not be able to approach Jesus physically face to face, but I just believe that our posture to God in prayer should be just as Jairus' approach to Jesus in person. When you don't care who is around you watching, or when you don't care about your social, professional or clerical status or when you're not concerned about what you're wearing, that's when God can deal with you. Come in your brokenness. Come in your lowest state. Come to God drained of answers yet full of hope and expectations. Come to God with your seemingly impossibilities knowing that He can make them definite possibilities. Come to Him just recognizing that He is God. Psalm 100:3 (NKJV) says "know that the Lord, He is God..." Don't be so quick to go asking God for something. Instead, open up your approach knowing that you're coming to someone who is greater than all. God loves and He hates. God has joy, yet He hurts. God is pleased, yet He can be displeased. God is more than just an ATM where we come to make a withdrawal. God wants us to put time into recognizing who He is and what He wants. God wants you to know that as much as He knows about you, He also wants you to get to know Him.

Jairus came ready to give Jesus everything that was going on with him and concerning him. However, Jairus knew it was necessary for him to go from an erect position into a prostrate position. A prostrate position was an appropriate position seeing that he was in the presence of God in the flesh who has been famed all over as a miracle working man who taught as one with authority. Jairus was also in a place of hurt and desperation. Life has taken a toll on his daughter which has, in turn, taken a toll on him. His options are limited and there's no one else that can help in the area where he needs help. Sometimes life has a way of directing us to God because we've tried everything else and nothing else seems to work. However, if I'm aware that Jesus is a man who has done such extraordinary, unfathomable things that can't be explained then why not try Jesus? We've always heard people say that Jesus ought not be a 2nd or 3rd choice. Has it ever crossed one's mind that when you don't know nothing else, you do what you know to do? Many times, people won't try Jesus because of Jesus' adopted sisters and brothers – I'm talking about saved people like you and I. We keep forgetting that we didn't come into this world as Christians. We weren't born with communion wafers and vials of grape juice in our hands. We grew up learning how to do life carnally. Jesus hasn't been the first choice for many of us who were at one point not saved. We lived our lives as best as we knew how and took minimal risk. The risk increased once we came to learn about God and His Son Jesus and how faith plays an intricate role in the lives of believers. Now that we've connected to God through Christ, we're learning how to grow in the unity of the faith from glory to glory and from faith to faith. The walk of a Christian believer is an ongoing walk as well as a maturing walk. We shouldn't quickly disqualify people from knowing Jesus because the women can't wear pants in church or the men don't have a shirt and tie. Establishing a relationship with God starts from us inviting the unsaved to learn who Christ is and how He was sent to sacrifice His life for those who had yet to be saved. Jesus didn't wait for the world to get it right. In fact, the world still isn't right and Jesus has died, been buried, rose again, has all earthly and heavenly power and sits on the right hand of God and the world still hasn't gotten it right.

Before we get too caught up on how people should live and dress, we should prepare them on how to posture themselves to receive Jesus into their lives as Jairus did before he made his desperate request. Jairus came ready to revere and worship Jesus. Here's a question: If Jesus showed up right where you are right now, what would be your first reaction? It's a question you can't really answer right away because it's Jesus. You don't want to say the wrong thing or do the wrong thing. That's the right response. When we approach God in prayer or in worship of any sort, you don't want to approach him in any kind of way. You want to be respectful, yet anxious in His presence. You want to be at your best behavior, yet apologetic in your appreciation for what He has done in your life as well as who He is and has been in your life.

Let's look at David in Psalm 51 as a case study in his approach to God during a low period in his life.

Psalm 51 is a result of what had conspired in 2 Samuel chapters 11-12. David causes the death of Bathsheba's husband, Uriah the Hittite. He's already impregnated her without Uriah's knowledge of it and David moves her in his home and God is displeased with his actions. After David is rebuked by the prophet Nathan for his sinful acts, God also speaks through Nathan to David concerning the consequences of his actions. Turmoil would strike David's household, his firstborn child to Bathsheba would die and David would find himself in a place of hurt, grief and sorrow. Mind you that David is fasting for the child and pleading with God that the child would not die. Once the child had died David's servants were unsure as to how they would break the news to David and how he would receive the news seeing that he fasted, pleaded with God and stayed on the ground while the child was alive. As David perceived from the whispering of his servants that the child was dead, he washed himself, anointed himself, clothed himself, went to the house of the Lord and worshiped. Then he went to his house, requested food and ate (2 Samuel 12:10-20).

Now, we have a warrior and a king who has sinned before God and man. He has tricked and schemed and has found himself suffering for his wrong. Yet, even in being rebuked for his sin, he doesn't use his position as king and his power as a warrior to override his posture before God. In Psalm 51 David doesn't present his position, power and prestige before the Lord. Instead, he presents himself as one who has fallen and presents himself to the one who is able to deliver him, cleanse him and restore him. Let's take a look at this psalm and review David's posture and presentation before the Lord:

> *Have mercy upon me, O God, according to thy lovingkindness: according*
> *unto the multitude of thy tender mercies blot out my transgressions. Wash*
> *me thoroughly from mine iniquity, and cleanse me from my sin. For I*
> *acknowledge my transgressions: and my sin is ever before me. Against thee,*

thee only, have I sinned, and done this evil in thy sight: that thou mightest be justified when thou speakest, and be clear when thou judgest. Behold, I was shapen in iniquity; and in sin did my mother conceive me. Behold, thou desirest truth in the inward parts: and in the hidden part thou shalt make me to know wisdom. Purge me with hyssop, and I shall be clean: wash me, and I shall be whiter than snow. Make me to hear joy and gladness; that the bones which thou hast broken may rejoice. Hide thy face from my sins, and blot out all mine iniquities. Create in me a clean heart, O God; and renew a right spirit within me. Cast me not away from thy presence; and take not thy holy spirit from me. Restore unto me the joy of thy salvation; and uphold me with thy free spirit. Then will I teach transgressors thy ways; and sinners shall be converted unto thee. Deliver me from bloodguiltiness, O God, thou God of my salvation: and my tongue shall sing aloud of thy righteousness. O Lord, open thou my lips; and my mouth shall shew forth thy praise. For thou desirest not sacrifice; else would I give it: thou delightest not in burnt offering. The sacrifices of God are a broken spirit: a broken and a contrite heart, O God, thou wilt not despise. ~Psalm 51:1-17 KJV

As we look at this psalm of David, we don't see any physical posture mentioned. However, we do see a posture of the heart. David is asking God to do several things that reach the heart of God. Things that cause God to move within the one who seeks Him to do internal work. Let's list some of the things in which David is asking God to internally do: 1) Have mercy on me 2) blot out my transgressions 3) Wash me thoroughly from mine iniquity 4) cleanse me from my sin 5) Purge me 6) Wash me 7) Make me to hear joy and gladness 8) Hide thy face from my sins 9) blot out all mine iniquities 10) Create in me a clean heart 11) Renew a right spirit within me 12) Cast me not away from thy presence 13) Take not thy holy spirit from me 14) Restore unto me the joy of thy salvation 15) Uphold me with thy free spirit 16) Deliver me from bloodguiltiness 16) Open my lips and my mouth shall shew forth praise (a praise that's inside). David is asking for a lot, but for the sin in which he performs, he realizes what's at stake – his fellowship with God. David's relationship with God means so much to him that he's willing to seek God in making sure that God isn't absent from his life. David wants to have joy again. He wants to have a mind that's been purified by God Himself and once he's able to experience the revival that only God can provide for him, he wants to be an example and lesson for others (Psalm 51:13) to not fall in the trap of thinking you can have what you want because of your place, power and prestige in life. It took an unpleasant word from God that led David to posture himself before God to seek the Lord for restoration, fellowship, purity and revival. David knew that if he came to God broken and beaten as well as humbled enough to recognize that God can fix him, then God would not despise his posture. David expressed what he was dealing with internally as a result of what he did externally. Sin was internally in David for him to perform it externally. However, his worship to God internally would be acknowledged if he expressed it externally. Does God know what's internally wrong with us? Of course, He does. However, when you're in relationship with Him, there has to be communication that acknowledges God as Lord of our lives. David knew that he could not fix himself nor solve his own sinful issues. Therefore, he goes to his God that can fix what he couldn't.

Jairus has this encounter with Jesus knowing about His fame and wondrous works. He knows that Jesus isn't just another man. This was someone who brought about change in a way that has never been seen before. Jairus knew that not just anyone could help him. Jairus' problem wasn't a result of a sin problem. His problem was clearly a result of being a witness of what Jesus can do when they surrender to His plan. As we continue in this faith walk, we move from Jairus falling at Jesus' feet as a sign of submission and reverence to him presenting to Jesus something that represents what's been birthed from him. But, before we move forward, let's conclude this chapter with the understanding that anyone can physically show that they're in need of a miracle, but if your heart doesn't line up with your act, God won't be quick to move on your behalf. God isn't moved by what we simply do. He searches the heart. Psalm 139:23-24 (KJV) says *Search me, O God, and know my heart: try me, and know my thoughts: And see if there be any wicked way in me, and lead me in the way everlasting.* Psalm 51:16-17 NKJV says *For You do not desire sacrifice, or else I would give it; You do not delight in burnt offering. The sacrifices of God are a broken spirit, A broken and a contrite heart—These, O God, You will not despise.* 1 Samuel 16:6-7 (KJV) says *And it came to pass, when they were come, that he looked on Eliab, and said, Surely the Lord's anointed is before him. But the Lord said unto Samuel, Look not on his countenance, or on the height of his stature; because I have refused him: for the Lord seeth not as man seeth; for man looketh on the outward appearance, but the Lord looketh on the heart.* Before one seeks God in efforts of desiring something from Him, seek Him in investigating and testing your heart so that when it's in your heart for Him to do something for you or others, you're not asking with selfish or ill – will ambitions. We all have some things we desire from God, but if our motives and intentions aren't in line with what God wills for us, we might either be asking for the wrong thing, the right thing for the wrong reason or maybe even the right thing for the right reason in the wrong season.

Our posture before God is critical in our faith walk and we must be genuine and vulnerable before God to help us see our way through our issues enroute to the outcome that He's destined for our lives.

Chapter 6

WHEN WHAT I BIRTHED IS AT THE POINT OF DEATH

And besought him greatly, saying, My little
daughter lieth at the point of death...
Mark 5:23a KJV

Have you ever birthed something that took time and effort to develop just to see it die? You had an idea that would potentially become a business, a book or even a ministry that you poured your all into it, but something took place that caused it to dwindle away. Maybe you're a mother that was with child, but for some physical reason the child dies before they even enter into the world. I don't believe nothing in the world is more grievous than to lose a child. Even if the child was born, grew up, experienced life, yet, due to health reasons, violence, a freak accident or just in the process of life that child loses their life. Now the moments that you and that child had created together – whether young or old – have become memories and you'll never get the chance to ever hug them, kiss them, encourage them or even see them accomplish their life goals because they are gone. No concerned parent wants to see their child die before they do. It's a crushing blow to experience such a loss no matter who you are, what you do or how prestigious, positioned or powerful you are. Losing something or someone that's precious and meaningful to you can cause anyone to crumble to their knees. We've even seen famous people lose their lives through suicide and people like us on the outside looking in have the nerve to ask "what can cause someone like that to kill themselves?" "With all the money, the fame and power they possess, what could have made them do such a thing?" Being rich, popular, famous and powerful doesn't mean that you're not a recipient of being disturb by the cares of life. Everyone has a soft spot that, once pressed, it can rock us to our core.

Jairus, the ruler of the synagogue that called the shots concerning the protocol for synagogue worship, has now postured himself before Jesus with a problem that goes way beyond his title and power. He's not pompous in his encounter with the Lord nor is he grand like Naaman, the army commander, was with the prophet Elisha. Instead, like King David, he postured himself before Jesus hurting and desperate, yet, in reverence and honor. In his posture of humility and reverence, Jairus *besought Him greatly*. Simply put, Jairus greatly begged Jesus. This wasn't the begging of a man who's in the streets wanting some money to cater to a drug habit or an alcoholic desire. This was an astounding calling for Jesus to come and revive the life of a child in which a father has future hopes and dreams for. Jairus is desperately seeking Jesus to heal a child that he himself is making plans in life for. This father has probably invested time to see this child become someone great to now witness the possible decline of her life altogether. He hoped to see his daughter become a future wife and bear his future grandchildren. He longs to be the father that gives his daughter's hand to another man in holy matrimony and kisses her cheek to display how proud he is to witness such an amazing moment, but now she lies at the point of death.

For someone to lie at the point of death, the doctors have done all they could do. They've treated her as best as they could and now, she's in the fight for her life. Her chances of survival are low and this father has made the press to leave from his daughter's bedside to seek after the man whose name has been spread abroad for performing miracles. Prior to chapter 5 we've witnessed Jesus heal sicknesses and diseases as well as cast out devils and preach with authority unlike any other. Now Jesus is met with a situation where a child could die. Yet, this father who makes haste in reaching Jesus has ignored his hierarchy, pomp and grandeur to receive help for his dying daughter. This father sees an emergency of possible life expiring. He doesn't wait until death sets in. He makes haste to get the help she needs. Many of us as believers can over spiritualize our own lives by acting as if there's no need to rush to do anything. We'll simply say "let's pray." "God has the final say." We can be naïve at times concerning human nature. People respond differently when trouble comes. We all have ways on how we deal with problems. Some may result in drinking, drug usage, fighting, smoking, so on and so forth. When it comes to possible death, we move to action. We call who we have to call and try our best to assess the situation as best as we can. Jairus could've sent servants to seek out Jesus concerning his daughter, but Jairus took matters into his own hands and made up in his own mind that if anybody is going to reach out to Jesus concerning a problem beyond his reach, it's going to be Jairus himself. No one can explain his daughter's dilemma better than him. He knows how bad it is and the journey from how it started and how it is now. Later in the text we can assume that Jairus made sure that the right people were by the bedside of his child, such as the child's mother. You could say that it's alright to ask someone to pray for you, but allow me the liberty to simply say that there's nothing like establishing your own relationship with the Lord. The news media may only share what they know based on the reports they've received, the interviews they've facilitated and the research they've sought out. Nonetheless, no one can tell it like it is like the ones who were actually involved. I look forward to going to God concerning what I'm going through (even though He already knows). I look forward to sharing my life with Him knowing that He knows how to receive me and hear my heart's cry. My day is more fulfilling knowing that I've spent time in the presence of the Lord. Most of all, I'm sure that when I go to God with any circumstance, I know that He has the answer to help me solve it.

Remember what David said concerning what God doesn't turn away in Psalm 51:17 NKJV. *"The sacrifices of God are a broken spirit, A broken and a contrite heart—These, O God, You will not despise."* When we find ourselves in a place where something or someone connected to us is at the point of emergency to the extent that they could be separated from us, we dig deeper than we've ever dug to make sure that things keep going strong. We become intercessors, if you will, for them. We push for them when they cannot push for themselves and get them the help they need to be whole again. We call on the Lord if we see that they may not have the wherewithal or the ability to call on God themselves. It may not be a matter of physical life or death, but it could be a matter of win or lose, reward or consequences or maybe even blessing or curse. When people or things connected to us are not able to do it for themselves, there's a pressing in us that can't just sit there and let it die. We have to do something. Jairus, being a concerned father who couldn't just sit there and accept life for what it was presenting to him, he decided that he would not settle for what life presented to him. If there is a possibility that life can progress on from what came from his own loins, he would seek out Jesus who would do something that others have never done that Jesus is known for doing. We as believers can't allow life to tell us what to accept as final. Our world is getting colder and colder. Relationships in family, marriage, ministry and community are dwindling rapidly and we're losing the foundations that kept things so solid. Our world is facing a spiritual decline where God is no longer God to them and Jesus has left us responsible to help redirect the world back to God.

All of us are Jairus in some way to someone or something. We can't sit and wait for what's close to us to just die. There must be an urgency to move into action for those who are at the point of death whether it be eternally separated from the Lord, missing out on the opportunity to deliver a soul from danger or the like. If you know someone who is at the point of losing it, don't determine that it's not your problem. Jesus says in Luke 19:10 (KJV) *"For the Son of man is come to seek and to save that which was lost."* Every soul that has yet to receive Jesus as Lord and Savior is lost. They're all at the point of being eternally separated from the Lord. That's nothing for any believer to be slow to move on. It's our Godly duty to act with urgency to help get saved those who are on the brink of not living forever with the Lord. Due to man's sin back in the Garden of Eden in disobeying God, every life thereafter was born into sin. It was nothing we did ourselves. It was inherited by us. We had no choice in the matter. However, we don't have to stay in that shape, which is why God sent His only begotten Son to this world. God loved us so that by sending Jesus that all who believe in Him shall have everlasting life (John 3:16). Unfortunately, those who have not been reached with the gospel have no idea that they're in spiritual danger of not being able to spend eternity with the Lord. Jesus didn't wait for us to "get it together" to die for our sins. He died while we were yet sinners or while we were missing the mark (Romans 5:8). Jairus can actually be a type of Christ by being the mediator for one who couldn't do it for themselves. Jairus sacrificed his reputation, his place in society and his religious hierarchy just to cater to the needs of one who was at the point of death.

Despite the current state of this world, it belongs to the Lord. Psalm 24:1 (KJV) says *the earth is the Lord's, and the fulness thereof; the world, and they that dwell therein.* This world is a part of God. He created it and all that's in it belongs to Him. We may have left

Him, but He never left us. We turned to wickedness, but God Himself never left. He's still waiting on us to get back to Him, but it takes a Jairus – type people to place their reputation to the side and focus on bringing the dying back to the Lord.

Before we progress to the next chapter ask yourself this: who or what is at the point of death or great consequence that you must urgently seek the Lord to determine how to deliver them or it from being expired? Who or what needs to be nourished and cared for to live beyond their dilemma? Is there someone you know that has no idea on how to conquer life and you know they're in need of deliverance? If you can't think of anything or anyone, that calls for immediate concern on how you view the world and its current condition.

Chapter 4
LORD, CAN YOU COME AND DO IT LIKE THIS?

I pray thee, come and lay thy hands on her, that
she may be healed; and she shall live.
~Mark 5:23b KJV

People are different and unique in their own individual way. Our style, our character and our way of life varies from one another in so many different ways. My family (especially my sister), to this day, pokes fun at me on how I eat my food. I never really paid much attention to it myself so I never really saw it as something worth digging into. Whenever I would have a plate of food, I would eat each item on my plate one entrée or side at a time. I guess it's all about holding on to that flavor until that food item is no longer on my plate and I simply move on to the next item. My sisters would joke and mess with me about it, but in the end, that's how I eat. Every once in a while, I would pause in the middle of eating one item and go to the next. Yet, I will eventually go back to that item. It's not a big deal on the order in which I eat my meal. As long as I get to enjoy the meal that I've been longing for. You work all day longing for a specific meal thinking about how good it's going to taste once you've been able to sit down and just rest in a place of good tasting food to satisfy your appetite. Think about that young child who is living in poverty, whether in a third – world country or right in your own community, and think about if they are concerned about being picky or peculiar about their meal. They can care less about the trimmings or the food touching. They're just grateful to eat something.

Jairus, the synagogue leader, is in a place where his daughter is lying at the point of death and his power, position and prestige can't help him. Yet, he sees Jesus and postures himself to seek the help that his daughter needs. He doesn't go into detail about him being a prominent synagogue leader who belongs to a specific religious sect. That stuff doesn't matter to him. The only thing that matters to him is that Jesus can come and heal his daughter. Not once does Jairus offer money to Jesus or any type of incentive to come and heal his daughter. One can only assume that with the fame of Jesus' name and deeds being spread abroad, Jairus knew that Jesus wasn't moved by finances and other material wealth. He knew that Jesus was a man of compassion that was willing to assist those who were in dire need. Jairus wasn't a poor man who struggled with wealth. He was a well-off man who was rocked to his core at the knowledge of his dying daughter. Let me interject this small, yet powerful statement: You don't have to be a poor, poverty stricken individual to have your life altered by calamity. You can be in the best financial place in life and still have your life changed by one life changing moment that could potentially shake you to your core. Though I digress, we return to the fact that Jairus' societal status doesn't get Jesus' attention. It was posture and need that does. Jairus is open, honest and humble in his approach to Jesus concerning the current health dilemma of his daughter.

As Jairus shares the current status of his daughter to Jesus, he's also specific as to how Jesus can heal her. Jairus says to Jesus these words: *I pray thee, come and lay thy hands on her, that she may be healed; and she shall live* (Mark 5:23b KJV). Let's be careful how we break down the request from Jairus because Jairus isn't coming to Jesus in an arrogant, pompous presentation. Jairus is moving in haste, shaken to his core, ran out of sensible options and, foremost, he's a parent who is moving expeditiously on behalf of his dying daughter. He begs of Jesus greatly to, first, *come and lay hands on her.* Jairus is greatly begging Jesus to perform a miraculous act based on what he probably knows or heard about Jesus concerning healing ministry. Was he wrong for asking Jesus to do it this way if that's the only way he's familiar with? Of course not. Jairus should be commended that he looks to Jesus – period! Once again, we must be knowledgeable of the fact that God will not despise a broken heart who is desperate for Him and what He has to offer. The good news is that the word has been spread of who Jesus is and what Jesus was doing. I don't know about you, but that sounds to me like the good news of Jesus and a life who is desperate in seeking Him because of the good news shared about Him – in other words, the gospel. Based on what Jairus knew about Jesus, he simply begged Jesus to do something that he heard Jesus was known for doing. I feel sorry for people who put down other people who are trying their best to utilize what they know about Jesus, even if what they know is very little. Just because I assume that you don't know any more than I know, does that mean that that person who knows little is at a disadvantage? I've been discipling a young man at the church I attend at the time of this book being written and I never assumed what he knew about Jesus. However, he knew that he needed God in a great way and I commended his growth no matter how little or much he knew. The truth was that when he rightly applied what he knew and received what he was supposed to receive, God would get the glory. Jairus begged Jesus to come and do something that Jesus was known for doing. Do we know what Jesus can do? If so, should we be concerned as to how He would do it? Jairus had no clue in terms of if Jesus was going to do it at this point. He hoped that Jesus would come and heal his daughter in a way that was made known to him. His total confidence was based on what he knew Jesus could do. This was not a matter of *if Jesus did for others, He would do it for Jairus.* Jairus knew what Jesus could do based on the witnesses of others. Now, it was a moment for Jairus to take what he knew or heard about Jesus and hope that Jesus would do the same for his daughter.

Here's another fascinating item about Jairus' request. After he asks Jesus to come and lay hands on his daughter, his expectation of doing what he begs of Jesus is concluded that *she **may** be healed; and she **shall** live.* Notice that the word *may* is not connected to the word *be.* The word may in its usage is a verb used in the way to have permission or to be allowed. It also means to be strong or have power. This is different from the word *maybe* which means chance or possibility. Jairus was not suggesting that if Jesus came and laid hands on her that there is a possibility that she may be healed. Jairus' hope rested upon the fact that based on his request, his daughter will be healed. Making such a statement requires great faith beyond human reasoning and medical knowledge. Making such a statement doesn't dilute one's knowledge, training and experience of all things medical, but it simply places one's trust in something or someone greater than the human and medical logic. Jairus had enough faith in Jesus' work that he may have never seen with his own eyes. Yet, based on what he knew, it was enough to trust Jesus that once Jesus does what He does, that his daughter would receive what Jairus had begged for. Not only would she be healed from her sickness, but Jairus adds that *she shall live.* The word *shall* is a verb used before another verb to indicate the simple future tense, particularly in the first person singular or plural. Also, used similarly to indicate determination or obligation, particularly in the second and third persons singular and plural. Jairus believed in the power of Jesus so much that once Jesus did his task, then the young girl would be healed and the future of the girl would be that she would live. It's one thing to believe God for yourself, but to believe God beyond yourself and not knowing what the suffering individual is feeling shows a trait of selfless love and commitment to seeing others be lifted up.

We have to be a people of faith, hope and love that when we see the current condition of the world we live in, we have to look outside of ourselves and see that people need Jesus more than we know. Jairus saw the condition of his child, but he didn't know about it firsthand. Even though he hadn't experienced what his daughter experienced, it didn't stop him from interceding for his daughter. Jairus may have moved on what little he knew about Jesus, but the blessing is in acting on what you do know for the sake of saving the life of another. Don't belittle people who haven't been a member of the church as long as you have. Don't stifle their growth in God because of their limited knowledge of Psalm 23 and the Model Prayer. Instead, celebrate their learning to know what they need to enhance, develop and grow in their relationship with God.

Before we enter into the next chapter, I want to expand your level of knowledge concerning how God works. Jairus asked Jesus to come and lay hands on his daughter so that she may be healed and shall live. Is it possible that Jesus may not have healed her in the way that Jairus described? Could it be that God wants us to grow beyond how we think He should work? There are so many ways that Jesus impacted the lives of people concerning their physical health that time would not allow me to share. Jesus didn't have to come nor did he have to lay His hands on Jairus' daughter. That's not what this is about. It's simply about looking to Jesus when we need Him. We should never be caught up in the "how" of Jesus to the extent that if He doesn't do it "how" we want Him to do it, then it could derail our faith in terms of Him being able to do it. Think about what we discussed about Naaman and how he wanted to be healed from leprosy. It had nothing to do with how he wanted to be healed. It was his ability to look past his power, position and prestige to see that his deliverance was in trusting and believing God through the instruction of the man of God and being obedient throughout the process. Jesus says in Mark 9:23 (NKJV) *"If you can believe, all things are possible to him who believes."* If we were to get caught up in the "how" of God, then it's possible that we can become stagnant or even stationary in the process of playing our part. There will be moments when our "how" and God's "how" will differ. It doesn't mean that God is against your request, sometimes it's just a matter of God developing you in His "how."

Nonetheless, we continue on seeing that Jairus' request has pushed him to believe that Jesus would respond to his request based on what he knows about Jesus and having the confidence to believe that once Jesus has done his part, healing and life will spring forth.

Chapter 5
JESUS IS COMING, BUT WHY THE CROWD?

And Jesus went with him; and much people
followed him, and thronged him.
~Mark 5:24 KJV

As we continue this journey of faith, we find Jairus in a vulnerable state where he has set aside his position, prestige and power to cater to the needs of his dying daughter. He's postured and positioned himself in a way that a person who is desperate for an answer can do so. He's not fixated on an issue of his own, yet the need is concerning one who is connected to him. He's been made aware of Jesus' coming as well as Jesus' ministry and he's hoping that Jesus can produce another miracle in a way that's been known to him. He's not rushing Jesus to make a move, but he's desperate for something to happen for his daughter. As a result, Jesus decides to go with him. Oh, how relieved Jairus must be to finally have Jesus make his way to his dying daughter. We're not made aware of the background as to other methods Jairus resulted into trying to get the help his daughter needed. We're not even sure if her case may have been a simpler case to be fixed that, over time, had gotten worse due to the lack of needed treatment. Nevertheless, Jairus has now acquired the help of Jesus to come and get the help his daughter truly needs.

As we see that Jairus gets Jesus to come and see about his daughter, the narrative shares with us that *much people followed him and thronged him* (Mark 5:24b KJV). Based on the flow of the text, these were those who have been following Jesus probably since chapter 4 after Jesus had been teaching as well as others who have been following him after the great storm (vv. 35-41) along with those who witnessed the deliverance of the man who was demon – possessed (5:1-20). Now, the crowd has continued to follow Jesus and Jairus to see what Jesus was going to do next.

People have been following Jesus through His preaching and teaching as well as performing the great miracles, signs and wonders for others. These people haven't seen anything or anyone like Jesus before. A compassionate individual who is a freedom fighter for the oppressed, poverty – stricken and disenfranchised. He's concerned about people who have been looked over and looked passed. He's brought hope to struggling families who longed to look beyond their downtrodden, current realities that seemed to never cease. Many of them have been recipients of healed bodies, restored relationships and unexplained increases in finances beyond their imaginations. How can a person be a witness to the greatness performed by Jesus and stay away once they received what they wanted or needed? You'll be surprised by the mindsets of people who feel that what they are dealing with they shouldn't be experiencing. They believe with all honesty that as good of a person they are that they should not have been experiencing such suffering and cruelty. There are even those who feel that because they are who they are that they deserve to be blessed. Based on their own sense of goodness and humanity toward others, they feel entitled to the blessings that come to them. We can be such a hindrance to ourselves that we fail to understand that we're not recipients to God's goodness and righteousness because of who we are. We've even convinced ourselves that we don't have to be active members of a local fellowship to show how much we love the Lord. When God gives us something to hope after, we shouldn't posture ourselves to get it when we feel like it. We ought to be thirsty and desperate for whatever God has to bring to us. It's not by any goodness of our own that we receive the awesomeness of God. He loved us in spite of our false sense of psychology, philosophy, philanthropy or humanity. Romans 5:8 (NKJV) says: *But God demonstrates His own love toward us, in that while we were still sinners, Christ died for us.* God didn't bless us in this way because we deserved it. He blessed us because we needed it and no one could have provided such a love like this other than God Himself through Jesus.

Jesus' fame has spread abroad concerning his ministry of compassion in action and people continue to follow Him onto the next moment of a life challenge. Why are the people following Him? 1) Some may be following Him because they were recipients of the life – change He brought to their lives. Jesus impacted their lives in a way that no one else has ever done before and to fall back would be an injustice. When someone has made an everlasting impact in your life in a way that no one else can ever come close to doing, there's a gratitude that has to be shown. You just can't stop at a singular – use of saying thank you. When you understand how urgent you needed the help you needed, it's only right that you show just as urgent an ongoing show of thanks. 2) Some may have followed Him to see if His compassion was constant. How can someone continue to show compassion to people who are in drastic need? Is it possible that Jesus had an "off day?" You'll be amazed at how much people are looking for a Jesus that they can relate to. What does a *tired* Jesus look like? What about a *frustrated* Jesus; an *irritated* Jesus; a *depressed* Jesus; or maybe even a Jesus that wanted to use profanity. There's no way that Jesus could be that compassionate about people and not get exhausted, burnt-out, annoyed or even mentally drained. The weight that comes with being compassionate is being able to know that you can't be there for everyone. Jesus sacrificed His own life so that mankind wouldn't have to pay the price for his own sin, but the opportunity to accept Jesus as the one who did it for us is still on us. Jesus can't worry about who doesn't choose Him. He did His part by being the constant, compassionate deliverer. 3) Maybe there were people who were looking forward to the streak of Jesus' performance of miracles coming to an end. Some people just don't believe that change can happen for them. They've been so conformed to seeing that they can't live beyond their place of stagnancy that there's no way it can happen for no one else. Even those who proclaim to be Christians doubt that there's no way they can do what Jesus did. Could it be that your job is not to do what Jesus did, but to do what Jesus said? Sounds like some false doctrine to me, but stay with me. God didn't send you to die for the sins of the world. That was Jesus' job. God didn't send you to marry a prostitute to symbolize how we walked away from Him, yet He still wants us as His. That was Hosea's job (Hosea 1). God didn't send you to part the Red Sea. That was Moses' job (Exodus 14). Don't be disappointed when you can't do what others have done. Jesus' miraculous acts isn't about doing what He did, but doing what He said. If He said you will tread upon serpents (things that are made to kill you), then be confident that you can do so. If He said you will lay hands on the sick and they will recover, have faith that when you lay your hands that people will recover.

The point that needs to be stressed is that we all need to be mindful as to why we are following Jesus. Many of us follow Jesus for the "stuff" we can get. Many of us follow Jesus because we've been convinced that life will be easier once we follow Him. Many of us follow Jesus because mother and/or father followed Him. There's nothing like a genuine relationship with God when you can testify to the fact that He brought a change and made an impact in your life that can't be touched. Our walk with Jesus should be a walk that includes knowing Him better (Philippians 3:10-14 KJV), learning from Him (Matthew 11:28-30 *The Message Bible*) and obeying Him (John 14:15 NKJV).

In the next portion of this faith journey, we'll discover something called *thronging*. As Jairus continues his desperate walk with Jesus, they both run into another life challenge where the crowd could either stagnate Jairus' need or show him how Jesus has everything under control despite a diseased woman and a thronging crowd.

Chapter 6
I WAS HERE FIRST!!!

And a certain woman, which had an issue of blood twelve years, And
had suffered many things of many physicians, and had spent all that she
had, and was nothing bettered, but rather grew worse, When she had
heard of Jesus, came in the press behind, and touched his garment. For
she said, If I may touch but his clothes, I shall be whole. And straightway
the fountain of her blood was dried up; and she felt in her body that she
was healed of that plague. And Jesus, immediately knowing in himself
that virtue had gone out of him, turned him about in the press, and said,
Who touched my clothes? And his disciples said unto him, Thou seest
the multitude thronging thee, and sayest thou, Who touched me? And he
looked round about to see her that had done this thing. But the woman
fearing and trembling, knowing what was done in her, came and fell down
before him, and told him all the truth. And he said unto her, Daughter,
thy faith hath made thee whole; go in peace, and be whole of thy plague.
~Mark 5:25-34 KJV

Jairus, a desperate father who has begged and pleaded for the services of Jesus to come
and see about his dying daughter, has finally gotten Jesus to go with him to lay hands

on his dying daughter so that she may be healed. What a joy to know that Jesus is going to see about his daughter. Think about how excited he is. Think about how humbled he must be. Think about his unsurety of what's going to happen or what Jesus is going to do. The suspense is just too much to comprehend. One thing seems apparent though – that Jairus is relieved knowing that Jesus is going with him to fulfill a need that was beyond his control. There had to be some sigh of relief from Jairus. Who knows how long Jairus' daughter had been dealing with her illness and how long Jairus sought help for his ailing daughter? I wonder how Jairus' mother may have felt and what measures she has taken to get the help needed for their daughter. Despite the background prior to Jairus meeting Jesus, Jairus is going forth with Jesus to see about his dying daughter. But wait!!! There's another situation that arises as Jesus and Jairus are making their way to Jairus' house.

The bible shares with us that there was a certain woman who had a physical health issue concerning the flow of her blood – a hemorrhaging of blood – for twelve years (Mark 5:25). According to the Message Bible, she had been treated badly by many physicians or had endured much suffering at the hands of many physicians and spent all of her resources just to be in worse shape than she was before (Mark 5:26, *Amplified*). However, she hears about Jesus – who, of course, is with Jairus who eventually is on the way to save his dying daughter – presses her way through the crowd that's behind Jesus and touches His garment (Mark 5:27). Without a prior conversation with Jesus, she reasons within herself that if she can just touch His clothes, then she shall be made well (Mark 5:28). Once again, without a conversation with Jesus asking permission to even have a conversation with Him, she's immediately healed from her painful, uncontrollable blood flow of twelve grueling years and she was certain that she was healed from her affliction (Mark 5:29). Let's grasp what has taken place here. She's a woman. In those days, women didn't have much equality with men. They weren't known to just force their way into the presence or conversation of men. Next, she's a diseased woman. When a woman had a condition such as this woman in the text, she wasn't even supposed to be in the public. Back in Leviticus 15:25-27, if a woman had a flow of blood other than her menstrual period or her flow exceeded beyond her normal flow, she was considered unclean as well as those whom she had touched. Some may consider this woman to be reckless and irresponsible. To her, she didn't want to be exposed because of her issue. She had heard about Jesus and based on what she heard, all she wanted to do was get the help she longed for. She knew that no one else could help her and all her resources had been exhausted. Plus, she probably had no idea when she would have the opportunity to have an encounter with Jesus that could change her life forever. Her desperation and determination for change pushed her ahead of Jairus' dying daughter. She wasn't concerned about the laws of purity or the view of others. All she wanted was a chance to try Jesus for herself. No one told her if touching Jesus' clothes would change her situation. Where would she even get that line of reasoning from?

Jesus realized that something happened that caused power to be drawn from Him. This probably wasn't the first-time people touched his clothes, but this touch was different. This was an intentional touch. This was an uncommon touch. This was a meaningful touch. It was this kind of touch that would call for somebody to speak up and testify about what this touch had done for them. As a result of this power – drawing touch, Jesus turned toward the crowd and asked "who touched My clothes?" (Mark 5:30 KJV). Jesus knew exactly what He was asking. He knew that this woman wasn't the only one touching Him. Nevertheless, He also knew that no one could touch Him like that woman did. However, His own disciples failed to discern Him to determine who it was that touched Him the way He was touched that power was drawn from Him. His disciples turned to Him saying that Jesus sees a multitude of people *thronging* Him and yet He's asking who's touching Him (Mark 5:31 KJV). What the disciples failed to understand was the question that Jesus was asking. He wasn't asking who was *thronging* Him. He was asking who *touched* Him. The word *thronging* from its Greek translation meant "to compress" or "to crowd on all sides." When Jesus asked who touched Him, he wasn't asking who crowded his space or compressed His ability to move. He was asking who touched me to the extent that you pulled from within me something that was of great worth. She was able to pull something from Jesus that was dynamic in worth and ability. Jesus looks around to see the woman who was able to extract such power from Him, but she was in fear, yet willing to come and fall at the feet of Jesus to share with Him what happened and the summary of her life story (Mark 5:32-33). Jesus never condemned her from ignoring the purification laws nor did He interrupt her to tell her that He had another appointment to fulfill. He didn't tell her how she was increasing her risk of infecting other people. Instead, Jesus acknowledges her faith in Him that has caused her to receive the healing she longed for and sends her on her way to live in the healing from her affliction (Mark 5:34).

Why would we take this time to talk about ten verses of someone else's life challenge when Jairus has a dying daughter that needs to be catered to? What made this diseased woman a priority that she would desperately press her way to get healed when she was in the way? Was Jairus supposed to touch Jesus' clothes and take whatever power he absorbed from Jesus and heal his daughter? Jesus didn't just give the woman what she needed. She took it! She could've just waited because Jairus came first.

Sounds like us, doesn't it? "We've been at this church longer than anybody else. What makes them think they can just come in here and change stuff?" "I've been in the choir longer than they have. Why didn't they make me section leader?" "I've been an associate minister here longer than they have and can preach better than they can. What qualifies them to be the next Pastor?" I WAS HERE FIRST! We can act so entitled about things sometimes. Whether in the family, in business, in ministry or in life. Life isn't about being first. It isn't about having seniority or more experience. Life is a journey full of lessons to be learned. It's not about what we feel we deserve because of status, legacy or tenure. Jairus has Jesus by his side to fulfill a need. Jesus never left him to see the need of another. Jesus decides to help Jairus while indirectly helping someone else on the way. Notice that the woman was "on the way", not "in the way." Also notice that Jairus wasn't tossed to the side. Jesus was still by his side.

In a world filled with billions of people, what makes you "first?" Let's look at the truth of the matter. God loved the world so much that He gave us Jesus. The world doesn't just consist of you or me. It consists of all of us – past, present and future. You may have been born first, but God loved us all first. I may have been born last, but God loved us all first. He doesn't love me more than He loves you or vice versa. He loves us all with unconditional love. If God blesses you with a new career before He heals me from cancer, that doesn't make your blessing first or more important or even more urgent. The lesson that we should take away from this is that if God allows me to see you blessed before He blesses me, I'm hopeful knowing that He will bless me. In fact, I'm already blessed to see you blessed so that I can learn how I can be blessed also. I'm not sure what Jairus was thinking or feeling when this woman received her healing from Jesus. One thing that can be certain is that Jairus has now gotten a front row seat of seeing what Jesus can do instead of hearing about it. Jairus now has some evidence that Jesus can perform miracles. Someone else's desire to be healed was fulfilled and Jairus didn't have to witness the hearing of their prayer to discover how and why. Jairus saw firsthand what faith in Jesus can do when you forsake what others will say or think to seek after what's miraculous. Up to this point, all Jairus knew was "come lay hands on my daughter so that she may be healed and live." What he witnessed for himself was that "if I can touch what's connected to Jesus, I'll be made whole!"

What are you touching that's connected to Jesus? What scripture are we touching and agreeing with to believe God for something miraculous in your life? What individual have you connected with to pull God's best from for your life? Can someone connect with you because they see Jesus in you? Instead of you complaining about "I was here first", tell yourself that "I'm here!" You may not be first, but you're here! You may not be next, but you're here! You may not be ahead, in front, the tallest, the strongest, the bravest or the boldest. The good thing is that you're here!

Chapter 7

JAIRUS, I'VE GOT SOME BAD NEWS…

While he yet spake, there came from the ruler of the
synagogue's house certain which said, Thy daughter is
dead: why troublest thou the Master any further?
~Mark 5:35 KJV

Before Jairus had gotten Jesus to go with him, Jesus healed a demonic man. After Jairus had gotten Jesus to go with him, Jesus heals a diseased woman. Now that Jesus has healed the demonic man and the diseased woman, we continue on to see about Jairus' dying daughter. Jairus has shown such patience and humility so far. He had been hearing about what Jesus had done or what He could do. He forgets about his power, position and prestige and postures himself to seek help from the Lord. He presents his request to the Lord and Jesus agrees to go with him. He's witnessed a diseased woman who has risked it all to get her healing from Jesus without formally introducing herself while Jesus commends her for her faith in Him. Jairus has shown no signs of entitlement or pride while Jesus acknowledges this woman's faith. He has Jesus by his side and he can continue his walk with Jesus as he progresses with anticipation of Jesus healing his dying daughter.

While Jesus was speaking (to Jairus or the multitude is not certain), news came from Jairus' house concerning the current status of his daughter. "Your daughter is dead." The sword that pierces the heart of a desperate father. The very child that he helped bring into this world is now dead. His hopes and dreams for her have now been taken away by the delivering of four breathtaking words. What could be going through the mind of Jairus, the ruler of the synagogue? What is Jairus the father thinking? Could he be thinking that the woman who had the issue of blood was a waste of Jesus' time? That woman could've been in an isolated place recovering from her blood issue! We could've bypassed all this madness and we could've gotten to my daughter much sooner than this. And to make matters worse, someone is asking me why I trouble, bother or even worry the Master any further? Could these be things that Jairus is allowing to race through his mind? Up to this point, all Jairus has heard and witnessed for himself was in regard to those who were alive. What can Jesus do about my deceased daughter? Demonized men and diseased women were all that Jairus could go on. Jairus has never heard of Jesus raising dead people nor has he ever witnessed it for himself or even been the subject of such a thing. His daughter is dead and I'm questioned as to why should I trouble Jesus any further.

During the writing of this book our world has experienced a plague known as Covid-19 or the novel coronavirus. It's a respiratory, person-to-person infection that has become global. Hundreds of thousands have been infected and just as many have died as a result of it. Government officials have ordered citizens to stay home even to the extent that many of our local houses of worship have to close their physical doors to prevent the virus from spreading. Businesses have either shut down operations or readjusted their business hours and practices to keep their businesses afloat. Grocery store shelves are emptied out daily which has caused many to make good with what short resources they have. Young and old, black and white have been impacted by this devastating pandemic and the church-at-large is looking to determine what's next. It's times such as these that can cause anyone to say "why trouble the Master any further?" Even during a crucial time in our world's history, many of us are believing God like never before. We're live streaming Sunday worship services, we're having prayer conference calls during the week, we're finding creative ways to cater to the needs of the elderly and less fortunate while still having to meet the financial needs of the local house of worship. Some have come to believe that this is the beginning of the end for this world and it's only going to get even worse. If we then believe that things are going to get even worse than this, then what more can we do?

Even during a time when a global pandemic is sweeping our world like never before, we continue to trust God. Businesses are drifting, lives are taken away, jobs are declining and families are backed in a corner, but we as the body of Christ continue to believe in God, not just in what we say, but in what we believe and what we do. Jairus is at a crossroads. He's been told that his daughter is dead. He's also told that there's really no need to trouble Jesus any further than what he already has. Does Jairus prepare the funeral? Does he reach out to the undertaker and tell them that they can come and collect the remains of what used to be his daughter? Does he now carry-on life knowing that life has to go on with him and his wife not having a child to groom for life? How can we – the church – encourage others to press forward in life when we have been hit with a domestic blow ourselves? The world isn't the only one stricken with bad news. We, as believers, have moments that hit us at our core that can either silence us to tears and groanings or have us act out in rage asking God why. We could fall into a drunken stupor and self – medicate ourselves with drugs and alcohol to numb us from the reality of our losses or we can wipe the tears from our eyes and put God to the test by helping us maneuver through life's greatest horrors stories that have the potential to swallow us completely. Some of the most influential people in my life have passed from this life and I never imagined how life would be without them in my life. I was naïve to think that they would live forever. The parts that they have played in my life have been integral to my well-being. I wouldn't know where I would be without them. Mother Dorothy Smith hugged so many problems out of my life, but when she passed away, who would be able to replace her? Sis. Mattie Gillard was more than just a Sunday School teacher in the classroom, but she was a family friend outside the church house. She bought me my first basketball and took me to Fuddruckers where I can make my own hamburgers. My grandfather, James O. Burnett, Sr., was the patriarch of our family who for 95 years told us about getting to know Jesus, teaching us life skills and knew how to bring the family together. With these and others no longer in my life, how would I be able to get through life? It was after these losses that I began to learn that the more I lost, the more I had to gain. But what was I supposed to gain or who? They were tough lessons, but learned lessons. Every loss taught me how to look to God more. Whatever I lost in them, I gained in Him.

Now with Jairus having to face a life without the presence of his daughter, what does he do now? Does he prepare to bury the remains of his daughter and send Jesus on his way? As we progress into the next chapter, we learn that Jesus hears what's being placed in the atmosphere. Do we allow what's being placed in the atmosphere to alter our perception or do we allow Jesus to help us maintain our belief that things can change even in the face of loss?

Chapter 8
JESUS IS GOING WITH YOU FOR A REASON

As soon as Jesus heard the word that was spoken, he saith unto
the ruler of the synagogue, Be not afraid, only believe.
~Mark 5:36 KJV

For Jairus, his daughter is now dead. He sought after Jesus to prevent her death from even happening. He laid aside his place of power, prestige and position to seek after someone who could deliver his daughter from ever reaching the point of death. He was desperate, yet humble in his approach when seeking after the Lord. He gets Jesus to go with him, but on the way to Jairus' house, Jesus is touched by a diseased woman that has now recovered from her illness. Without Jesus directly doing anything, Jairus witnesses the power of Jesus in the life of this woman and Jesus acknowledges this woman's faith. However, after Jesus acknowledges this woman's faith which resulted in her healing, Jairus and Jesus progress their way to Jairus' house just to receive word that Jairus' daughter is dead. In fact, the messenger that sent word to Jairus doesn't even see the point of Jesus being there. In other words, Jesus should have been on His way. Nothing left to see here. Time to make funeral arrangements. There's nothing else that can be done…or is there? Many of us have been the recipient of bad news at some point. We lost money on a possible business venture; we've divorced from a 20- or 30-year marriage;

the doctor shares that there's nothing left to do except call the funeral director. Whether these or other life altering scenarios, we were the receivers of some bad news. A bad report has had the potential of rocking us to our core. We find ourselves in shock, at a standstill, devastated and even felt led to contemplating suicide or harming the lives of another or maybe even violating someone's property. We self – medicate with alcohol, drugs and even engage in sinful, sexual activity to help us numb the pain. Even if we don't do any of these things, we hurt and we cry. We become an emotional wreck with our countenance as cold as stone.

The very thing that we love, cherish and care for is gone. It's one thing to hear that your child / loved one is gone, but to hear that there's no longer a need for Jesus to be present can somewhat shake your faith in Him. You went through more than enough to seek after the Lord to now hear *"why troublest thou the Master any further?"* I can remember a time when I lost my aunt in 2014. I just lost my job and days later I hear of her passing. Even when my family and I received the news, I just had to see her for myself. I have to admit that the closer I walked to her bedside the slower that walk became for me. When I finally walked in that room with my mother and other family members, it was automatic for us to just cry. However, there was a moment while I was in that room that I stopped crying and under my breath I began praying that the Lord would raise up my aunt. I wasn't trying to be selfish in wanting to keep her here. It was just that she had been bedridden for so long and not able to speak on her own that I just wanted the Lord to deliver her from being so sick. I personally had nothing to gain from her living per se, but I wanted this to be a moment where God showed up just like I heard and read about in the scriptures. In other words, even in death, I was believing God to do what He has done for others to do the same for my aunt. What could have caused me to believe that God could deliver my aunt from death? What gave me the nerve to have faith in God that He could raise my aunt from the dead. Simply put: it was the word of God that I heard and read. With all the praying and believing I did in that room, God did deliver my aunt from her illness and allowed her to leave this world. Though I miss her even to this day, I believe that God gave her the release she needed. Even after her death, I still believed in God. There was nothing about her death that caused me to stop believing that God could and would deliver her.

Jairus went out of his way to seek after Jesus so that the Lord would deliver his daughter from death. However, even in the event of hearing about his daughter's passing, Jesus gives Jairus something that Jairus was originally looking for – hope. Even at the word of death, Jesus gives Jairus a word of consolation and a word of faith. *"Be not afraid"* was the word of consolation that spoke to Jairus' fear. The word afraid comes from the Greek word *phobeo* where we get our English word *phobia* which means to cause to run away, terrify or frighten. Jesus was simply telling Jairus not to allow what he heard to cause him to run away from his faith in Jesus. Don't be frightened by the news that you heard. He never told Jairus to not claim the death of his daughter. He just told Jairus not to allow the news of what he heard about his daughter to cause him to be terrified of what he originally hoped for. Many of us can be naïve in our faith by saying that "I don't claim that" or "I'm not speaking that over my family." The truth of the matter is that death has taken place in his household. I don't downplay the faith of people, but I do want to address how we turn a blind – eye to what we've experienced in our lives. I can remember a time I had a blown tire on the expressway coming home from downtown and as I was pulling over toward the shoulder, I was having a tough time removing the tire. No matter how much I kept saying "Lord help me", that tire didn't inflate itself, the tire didn't come off and not once did I say "I'm not claiming that over my tire." Bottom line, I called my uncle to come to my rescue to remove the blown tire and replace it with a spare tire. God can't help us unless we give Him something to work with. When I called my uncle to come and help me with my roadside circumstance, what comforted me was him saying to me "I'm on my way." We have to learn how to accept the circumstances that come into our lives so that God can give us a word that can comfort us on our way to the next phase. I believe that Jesus could've just gave Jairus a word to take back with him concerning his dying daughter so by the time Jairus gets back to his daughter, she would be healed like the faith found in the centurion in Matthew 8:5-13. Jesus could've prophesied to Jairus about his daughter dying and healing her after she has died. Nonetheless, Jairus is terrified concerning the news of his daughter, but Jesus comforts him with a word of consolation that puts Jairus in a place of preparation for the next phase: stay in faith.

God knows that we will run into scenarios that can emotionally cause us to make unwise decisions that will cost us greatly. Fear can cause us to be indecisive, stuck and forced into a tight space in our lives. It's in moments such as these that God is looking for us to look to Him to find out what we should do now. All of us have had moments that we lost a loved one and we had our time to mourn and grieve. Sometimes, we allow our mourning and grieving to take us to dark and estranged places. Even in lost relationships, some of us have emotionally decided to forget all sense of responsibility to later regret it due to financial losses, familial responsibility and so on. If I lost my job today, my financial obligations still have to be met, my health still needs to be intact and my life will continue to go on. You can't make wise decisions when you're captured in fear. Let's read what the Apostle Paul tells Timothy in 2 Timothy 1:7…

> *For God did not give us a spirit of timidity or cowardice or fear, but [He has given us a spirit] of power and of love and of sound judgment and personal discipline [abilities that result in a calm, well-balanced mind and self-control] (AMP).*

To help us learn how to operate outside of fear and terror, we must look to the Spirit of God who is the spirit of power, love, sound judgment and personal discipline. First, God wants us to learn how to operate in the capable ability to place our fear under submission (power). Second, He also wants us to operate in the act of doing what we need to do in contrast to doing what we want to do. For example, the word that Jairus heard about his daughter placed him in fear, but the word spoken from Jesus concerning his fear would now put Jairus in a place of controlling his fear so that he can continue having hope (love). Lastly, God wants us to operate in personal discipline by way of sound judgment so that we won't respond or act in fear (sound mind). So many times, we want God to do everything while we sit back and do nothing. In Luke 19:11-27 Jesus tells a parable about a nobleman and his ten servants. The nobleman gives each servant a portion of his goods with expectations of growing his investment. In verse 13 after he gives them his substance, he tells them all "occupy till I come" *(KJV)*. In other words, Jesus is expecting us to do something productive with what He has given us until His triumphant return. What's the purpose of us as Christian believers being left with God's word if we're going to operate in something that God did not give us? Fear blocks our ability to trust God beyond our human reasoning and logic. We can't operate in the realm of faith when fear has clouded our mind. Jesus is reminding us now, as he was with Jairus, to not be afraid of what you heard. Instead, allow faith to push you beyond what you heard that originally disturbed and frightened you – *only believe.*

In one verse, Jesus transitions Jairus from a spirit of fear to a spirit of faith. Jesus is preventing Jairus from allowing a seed to be sown into his life that has the potential of producing a crop of fear and terror. He wanted to bring a spirit of comfort into Jairus' life so that Jairus could be comfortable in cultivating a seed of faith that started when he first sought out Jesus. Jesus did not want Jairus' fear to interrupt his faith crop that was on the verge of sprouting. Jesus didn't want anything to choke up Jairus' seed of faith. Jesus knew what could've happened if Jairus would've continued in fear. Many of us have had a life of delayed success because of the fear that was sown into us from a past experience. We're afraid of trying, risking, investing, planning or even committing because we're afraid that this will happen or that will happen. Well, how do you know that this or that will happen? Do we really know what the outcome is? Did someone tell us what the outcome would be? Did we witness the downfall of others and now we won't even try? I understand that many of us play it safe just so we can get by, but at some point, we must step out of our space of comfort and safety to believe God beyond what's average and sane. We've all heard people tell us how irrational we are for going big, trying hard, pressing forward or reaching for the stars. Unfortunately, because of what *they said,* we stop trying, stop pushing, stop praying, stop believing, etc. As a result, we never get to see what could've been. We end up growing old wondering what life could've been and we become history lessons to a new generation by telling them *"You don't want to end up like me."*

What is Jesus saying to us today? I believe even now Jesus is saying unto us that He knows what we've been hearing. He knows that what we've been hearing has affected the way we believe or even stopped us from believing. He can't stop us from hearing what we've been hearing, but He can encourage us to hear Him beyond what's already been heard. The Apostle Paul would tell us what he told the church in Rome from the book of Romans 10:17 when he says *"So then faith cometh by hearing, and hearing by the word of God" (KJV).* Our hearts (the mind) need to be fed with the comfort and patience of God's holy word. There's a reason why the bible is called the "Holy" Bible. Its wisdom is beyond human reasoning and separate from the logic of this world. The contents within it are sanctified for a believing people to live by and a sinful people to be saved. If we continue to allow His word to fuel our spiritual man, we can conquer life's challenges from the inside out. Whatever has overwhelmed us, challenged us, tempted us, frightened us and even overpowered us, we must allow His word to mature us, compel us, convince us, convict us and fill us. That way we can press through the test of times and come out of our hardships stronger, wiser, more decisive and most of all a testimony that can attest to the allowance of God's word having a powerful influence in our lives.

Chapter 9

SETTING THE ATMOSPHERE

And he suffered no man to follow him, save Peter,
and James, and John the brother of James.
And he cometh to the house of the ruler of the synagogue, and
seeth the tumult, and them that wept and wailed greatly.
And when he was come in, he saith unto them, Why make ye
this ado, and weep? the damsel is not dead, but sleepeth.
And they laughed him to scorn. But when he had put them all out,
he taketh the father and the mother of the damsel, and them that
were with him, and entereth in where the damsel was lying.
~Mark 5:37-40 KJV

When I was a young child (and to be honest, moments when I had gotten older) I wanted to be involved or a part of groups where my peers were having fun. I wanted to blend in and be a part of a social status that was cool to be in. I wanted to be a part of some elite groups that would strengthen my networking and present opportunities to collaborate on some special projects. Even since my years of preaching there were moments where I wanted to connect and rub shoulders with those who were able to get me to another place of success that I've never experienced before. However, as I've gotten older and began to see how Jesus carried on with His life, He wasn't trying to be a part of an elite group. He wasn't trying to rub shoulders with people that could make His name great. Jesus wasn't trying to fit in a social group that was popular. He was God in the flesh. He was already different. Jesus came to do something that, to this day, I've never seen or witnessed another man do – die for the sins of the world. He came as a sacrificial lamb that would give His own life as a ransom for us all. Even while we were sinners, He died for us (Romans 5:8). Jesus, by Himself, came to impact the lives of all. He came to free the slave & bound the wisdom of the oppressor. He came to express love instead of law. He provided an escape for the sinner and rebuke to the religious. Jesus was a controversial man with an intentional platform. A woman is caught in adultery and the law says that she should be stoned to death, but Jesus says to her accusers *"He that is without sin among you, let him first cast a stone at her"* (John 8:7 KJV). Jesus came to challenge the mindsets of those who thought they had a hold on life & law just to discover that there was another side of life that had yet to be tapped into – Love. Jairus was a man of power, prestige & position, yet Jesus took the time to cater to the need that Jairus himself couldn't cater to. I'm sure that Jairus did all that he knew to do, yet whatever influence, power or money he possessed it wasn't enough to keep his daughter alive. So, the powerful, positioned & prestigious Jairus is found at the feet of Jesus hoping that the Son of God could do something that Jairus himself couldn't do. Jairus, like any other caring parent, relinquished all the pomp & circumstance to cater to the well – being of his daughter. His status couldn't keep her alive. The law couldn't stop her from dying. His network and elite status weren't enough to sustain the chances of living for his little girl. So, as the songwriter would put it: *"When everything else fails, I can go to the Rock!"*

Once Jesus has arrived at the house of Jairus, Jairus receives word that his daughter had died. It doesn't even make sense to trouble Jesus any further (Mark 5:35). Another word for *trouble* in this text is the word annoy or bother. Now that Jairus' daughter is dead, there was no need for Jesus to be bothered or annoyed with the matter. What could Jesus do with a dead body? Where there's no life, there's death. Yet, Jesus gives a word of encouragement & empowerment and tells Jairus not to be afraid, only believe (Mark 5:36). To encourage someone to not be afraid is to provide for them a confidence & comfort to feel secure in. To empower someone to believe in something or someone is to give them a foundation to stand on. Jesus gives Jairus a word that he can find comfort & security in as well as a foundation to stand upon. In chapter 8 we focused on the reason as to why Jairus was able to get Jesus to go with him. Jairus wouldn't have sought after Jesus if he didn't believe that Jesus was able to do something about his issue. He reverenced Jesus although Jesus wasn't a part of any elite group. Up to this point, Jesus's words & work have spread throughout the land. If he believed that Jesus was able to do something while his daughter was alive, should now death stop his belief? Even in death and fear, Jesus has yet to tell Jairus what His plan was going to be. However, part of the plan would consist of Jairus not living in fear while living in belief that Jesus could do something to cause Jairus to find comfort, confidence & security in Jesus.

Now that Jesus has prepared Jairus for what's to come, let's look at the individuals in Jesus' corner. Upon entering the house of Jairus, Jesus permitted no one to follow Him inside except for 3 men. Peter, James and John. Why were these men chosen to follow Jesus into the house? What made them so special that they were chosen to enter the house for whatever was going to happen? Jesus is God in the flesh. He knows all and sees all. There's nothing that Jesus isn't aware of. He was here before there was a beginning and because He is the ending, nothing can ever last beyond Him. Even though I'm not as wise & knowledgeable as Jesus, I'll just try to gather some evidence that could lead Jesus to bring in these three men. Peter was able to admit that Jesus is the Christ & Son of the Living God in Matthew 16:16 (KJV) and Jesus knew that only God the Father could have revealed or uncovered this truth to him. Anybody can say it, but Jesus knew how it came about. Peter, along with his brother Andrew, were found fishing in Matthew 4:19 (KJV) and Jesus calls them to follow Him to make them fishers of men. In that same chapter, brothers James & John were mending or repairing their fishing nets and Jesus also called them to follow Him and they left their boats to follow Him (Matthew 4:21-22 KJV). Peter & Andrew dropped their nets while James & John left their boats and their father to follow Him. These men left their jobs, their businesses, their sources of income and families to follow after a man they never knew. Peter & Andrew were brothers as well as James & John. Both sets of brothers started their new lives as disciples of Jesus and will go forth in ministry as well. How interesting it is for families to pursue after Jesus and learn from Him as well as serve with Him. Now these sets of brothers find new fellowship with one another as brothers in the faith serving alongside and learning from Jesus. Peter & John also were able to contribute to the work of the Bible with their own books (1 & 2 Peter, 1, 2, 3 John and Revelation). Peter, James and John were also men chosen to see Jesus transfigured in Matthew chapter 17 & Mark chapter 9. Finally, these same three men were with Jesus in the Garden of Gethsemane in Matthew chapter 26, Mark chapter 14 and Luke chapter 22. As fun as it was to give some tidbits on why I believe they were chosen, let's stay in the context of this narrative.

Once Jesus tells Jairus to not be afraid; only believe – along with Jairus – He only brings in with Him Peter, James and John. As they enter into the house, Jesus gives no instructions to these three men other than to follow Him. Normally, I'm a firm believer in not over-spiritualizing the text. Many times, we go overboard explaining and interpreting scripture that it ends up going over peoples' heads and you've missed a valuable moment in teaching the main idea of the text. However, in this text I can't help but notice what was said beyond what was said. Let's look at Mark 5:37 (KJV) again: *And he suffered no man to follow him, save Peter, and James, and John the brother of James.* Jesus wanted no one to follow Him except Peter, James & John. Now, literally speaking, Jesus only wanted these three men, along with Jairus to follow Him inside. But let's look at these beyond its literal meaning. The word *follow* in Mark 5:37 is slightly different from the one in Matthew 4:19. In Matthew 4:19 Jesus is telling Peter & Andrew to *come here continually* while in Mark 5:37 Jesus is saying *accompany me or join in together.* As Jesus is only allowing Peter, James and John to join Him inside, Jesus is still telling them to continually follow Him as disciples. These three men have been chosen to see Jesus in a way that's going to cause them to see Jesus as to how He does what He does and why He does it to whom He chooses to do it for. As much as I want to unpack all of this now, let's continue on and unpack it all later.

As Jesus is wanting only Peter, James and John to accompany Him inside, Jesus is met with lots of noise, crying and mourning (Mark 5:38). Public mourning in those times was loud and rowdy. You couldn't help but notice that something was wrong. There was even a moment where the cries of some became riotous. Many of you may have witnessed families that may appear overly emotional after a loved one had passed. During these moments everyone wants to be the go – to for support and/or encouragement. Many want to claim that they were closest to the departed. Everybody was the best friend. Then, there's the possible inheritance issues. Who's going to get the house, the car, the clothes, the jewelry, the estate and so on. In other words – riotous behavior. In all the noise, the crying and the mourning, who's asking about Jairus and his wife? Who's checking on them to see how they are? We're so impacted by the losses and the gains that no one is concerned about the in between. Nobody is asking about the ones in the middle who provided the life that has been taken away from them. Who's comforting the ones who provided for the life they can no longer provide for? Jairus has suffered a loss that they can't get back. Whatever plans they had for their daughter are no more. The only person that has taken the time to be concerned about their loss is Jesus. Only Jesus provides the words of comfort, confidence and security for this grieving father. Everyone else is just making noise, acting riotous and mourning out loud. Jesus begins setting the atmosphere for peace within this grieving father's heart. No miracle has taken place, but a moment of care and support was truly a great start. At this point Peter, James & John haven't said or did anything. Other than Jesus, these three men are doing a great job. Sometimes in loss and heartache, the best thing you can do is keep quiet. If you don't know what to say, say nothing. Sometimes it is just your very presence that people need during a tough time in their life. Sometimes they're just believing God that someone they love and trust can be there in their moment of grief and loss (cf. Romans 12:15). Though Jesus had a plan in play, He made it a priority to provide what was needed. Jairus and his wife needed someone to care about what they lost. Jesus showed compassion, not to a man with power, prestige and position, but to a father who lost his child. I challenge you today to learn how to be more of a support system than a superhero. No one needs you to save the day. Just learn how to be available and supportive. You're not the only one that can bring sunshine to a person's day. You're not always going to be the one that people go to for support. Accept that you're not going to be the go – to person all the time. I have family and friends that have experienced loss of some kind. However, I was okay not being the go – to person when things had gotten bad. I would, though, reach out by either phone or text to let them know that I'm concerned and hope that all was alright. Even if they didn't call me immediately, I made myself available just by caring enough to offer my presence. In time, wombs may heal. Until then, sit on the proverbial bench until you're called to step in and play your role.

In Mark 5:39a KJV Jesus is asking as to why are people keeping up all kinds of commotion and weeping. That's kind of condescending of Jesus, isn't it? A child of a prominent man had died. Better yet, a child who will never grow up to be what they've always aspired her to be has died. How about this? A future world changer has been taken away. Yet, Jesus has the nerve to ask why people are crying? I'm sure Jesus wasn't trying to be insensitive to the cries of the people… or was He? Let's not forget that Jesus knows us all. There's no emotion He can't identify and expose. If we can be transparent about what He's asking, Jesus is simply asking this: "What's the real reason as to why you all are making all this noise?" I, personally, wouldn't advise you to try this approach. Nevertheless, Jesus is polling the room at a very intense moment of mourning and mixed emotions. Instead of them having their "crybaby convention", Jesus needs to know who's really concerned about the parties who have really been impacted. I'm reminded of a song that says *"What did you come to this service for?"* Jesus wants to know why are you here acting like this? Then, just when you thought that wasn't enough, He tells the "drama delegates" that the young girl who just died isn't dead at all – she is sleeping (Mark 5:39b). Wow! Jesus just shut the whole convention down! First, you question their cries and now you tell them she's just sleeping? Now all the drama delegates began to ridicule Jesus (Mark 5:40 NKJV). The Amplified Bible says that they began laughing scornfully. They pretty much laughed Him down. They weren't laughing with Him. They were laughing at Him. Notice their countenance for a moment. Before Jesus entered, they were crying recklessly, but after Jesus polls the room, they're mocking Jesus. Notice that they're not speaking up on behalf of Jairus or his wife nor on the behalf of the deceased child. They're focused on making a fool of Jesus. Now, after all this, I'm led to believe that Jesus didn't do this so that He could know who the real supporters were and who were the phonies. I believe that Jesus did this to show Jairus who was really concerned about the plight of Jairus. I think this is a good place to say to you that in your faith walk, everyone that appears to be for you isn't. Some people just want to show how important they can be, how involved they need to be, how much attention they want to get and so forth. However, there are those who really want to see you whole and want to invest their time and energy in seeing you come out of your struggles a winner. They're not concerned about how much attention it will draw them. They just want to see you whole and healed. They're not looking to get information to spread about you. They're looking to see if there's anything you need to experience the comfort, confidence and security you need to keep on going forward.

Jesus was bold in setting the tone for a miracle to take place, preparing disciples on how to follow His example and provide what's needed in the lives of the brokenhearted. Jesus's approach in setting the atmosphere was bold in execution, but it provided results necessary for the miracle to take place. Jairus was given the opportunity for Jesus to set an atmosphere to see as to whether or not people would be what Jesus was to him. Jesus was a comfort to Jairus, not the people. Jesus was an encouragement to Jairus, not the people. Jesus brought a sense of security to Jairus, not the people. Jesus set the atmosphere for a miracle to take place, a good support system and a seed of faith to plant in Jairus. The people provided none of these things.

Jesus also gave Peter, James & John a portable classroom to watch, listen and learn from. They weren't quick to do or say anything that wouldn't be conducive at the moment. Their eyes were open to see wondrous things from Him. Their ears were open to hear His message in the midst of the mess. Their minds were open to receive the lesson that was presented. The only thing left for them to do was to keep their mouths closed. One of the most valuable lessons to learn about being a follower of Christ is to know when to speak and when to keep quiet. Don't speak too soon when Jesus is in the midst of teaching. Don't get so caught up in the details that you miss the meat of the message. Everything isn't always in the practice of a thing. It's in the principle. We get so caught up in what we do and how we do it that we miss out on why we do it. The way Jesus did things doesn't mean I have to do it that way. The principle speaks to why Jesus did it overall. With Jesus being our example, we have to look to His word to get proper observation as to what we see in His word, proper interpretation as to how we understand His word and proper application as to how we apply His word. In doing this, we can properly set the atmosphere in various scenarios we face in life just as Jesus did for Jairus. Jairus didn't know what to do, therefore He looked to Jesus. So, just as Jairus sought out Jesus on what to do, we must also seek out His word to assist us in what we should do. As a result of Jesus setting the atmosphere, Jesus saw the ridicule and scornful laughing and decided to clear the room of those who mocked Him. Jesus was able to progress forward despite the ridicule. That's a downfall for many of us. We can't seem to get past the scorn of others. We allow the ridicule of others to sway us from completing our God – given assignment. A grocery store chain like Walmart doesn't stop doing business because of a negative review from a customer. A successful restaurant chain like Chick-fil-a doesn't stop operating because of a differing religious belief. Your success isn't determined by the profit you accumulate. The true success of an individual is birthed from rising beyond the ashes even when people try to keep you burnt. In closing, I'm reminded of a story about my late grandfather who was a member of a church in the city of Brickeys, Arkansas. Since the inception of the building, it had been brought down 5 times due to devastating weather conditions. Despite the damage the building took, my grandfather was there to help rebuild it back to its glory. My grandfather, Deacon James Odell Burnett, Sr., passed away in 2019 leaving a legacy of rising above the ashes despite the contrariness of the times. He never wavered in his faith and he understood his assignment. I'm thankful for his life and inspired to do the same. I challenge you to set the atmosphere and make it conducive for a miracle to take place. Remove the unwanted noise that's not designed to encourage you. Learn from Jesus' example and know what to do when it's your time to set the atmosphere. Remember that you don't need to get too caught up in the practice, as long as you understand the principle. Practice gets me ready while the principle tells me why I should be ready. When I understand the *why*, I can better prepare for the *what, when, where & how.*

Jesus continues to show His three pupils on how to follow His example. Though Peter, James and John follow Jesus into a highly emotional, highly intense period of time, it doesn't change the fact that they are there to learn how to discern & set the tone for miracles to come forth. Even now, Jesus is exhibiting to us on how we can set the atmosphere for our own miracles to come alive. Everyone isn't destined to join you for every moment in your life. Some are there to learn from your godly example while some are there to remind you that they're not ready to conquer what was meant for you to conquer. Family members, friends and acquaintances can only go so far with you and you have to decide as to whether or not certain people can follow you until the end or just to a particular point. Jesus is calling on us as disciples to follow Him, not just for a specific moment in time, but for life. We need Him every step of the way to help us navigate through life. He'll equip us for the journey and even guide you on who can come aboard.

What a moment for Jesus' disciples to experience! What a time to be invited into an experience filled with death, doubt and mixed emotions. Have you ever encountered moments where emotions are high? Did people count on you to change the tone of the atmosphere that you were brought into? Were there moments when you had to evict certain people from your vicinity just so you can progress with what's next? Whether you know it or not, people are relying on the Christ in you to stand up and stand out. If they knew what to do, wouldn't they have done it by now instead of looking to you? Jairus couldn't fix the situation. The disciples had no clue what to do. The weepers and wailers were just there for show. God wants to perform a good work in you, but it's going to take your submission & obedience to God for the good work to come forth. Don't allow the moments, the mayhem or the multitudes to coward out your opportunity for Christ to show up and set the tone for a supernatural move of God.

As we go into this final chapter, we're going to discover that the way Jesus helped Jairus wasn't the way that Jairus had originally intended. Can you go into a situation seeking help in a particular way just to see it go another way that you originally intended?

Chapter 10

DON'T BACK DOWN WHEN JESUS
DOES IT ANOTHER WAY

And he took the damsel by the hand, and said unto her, Talitha
cumi; which is, being interpreted, Damsel, I say unto thee, arise.
And straightway the damsel arose, and walked; for she was of the age
of twelve years. And they were astonished with a great astonishment.
~Mark 5:41-42 KJV

What a rollercoaster ride of a story this has been. Let's review: a powerful man of religious status has a desperate need which consists of a dying daughter. Though he was a man of status, his status isn't enough to save his dying child. When all else fails, he seeks out Jesus and shows reverence unto Him with hopes that Jesus could come and lay hands upon his daughter. Jesus agrees to go with him, but along the way Jesus (followed by a crowd) helps a woman who is suffering from a hemorrhaging. While Jesus is dealing with this woman dealing with blood loss, Jairus' daughter is still at the point of death. Jesus' virtue is drawn from this diseased woman, yet Jesus takes the time to cater to the woman to remind her that it was her faith that has made her whole. After Jesus heals her and spends time with this woman, Jairus' daughter is still at the point of death. After Jesus departs from the no longer diseased woman, Jairus receives word that his daughter is now dead. It was even advised that Jesus would no longer be troubled by Jairus concerning the condition of his daughter seeing that she is now deceased. Jairus goes through all this trouble to get Jesus to come heal his once alive daughter to now be faced with her death. Though dead, Jesus provides hope for this grieving father and encourages him to not be afraid, but to believe. Jesus observes a crowd of weepers and wailers just to announce to them that this child isn't dead at all. In fact, she's just sleeping. The weeping and wailing crowd go from being a weeping crowd to a scolding audience. While the crowd is scolding Jesus, no one is consoling Jairus. Jesus is the only one that gives Jairus a hope that goes beyond a scolding crowd and a grieving father. Jesus polls the room to see who the fakers are and demands that they all exit the place. Only Jesus, Jairus and Jesus' three pupils progress inside where the dead girl's mother sits with her deceased child.

I can remember when my family received word that my aunt, Erma Burnett, had passed away. This woman was the most active aunt in my life. She's lived with us, helped raise us and overall was just an everyday part of our lives. She loved to travel and she loved her family as well as her extended family. Having to hear about her passing was overwhelming. The night of her passing my mother and I, as well as a few others went to her bedside to view her body until the funeral home came to get her. That took hours for them to come, but the trip to see her felt just as long. As we approached the rehabilitation center where she was, the walk inside seemed so long and slow. The lights in the building were low seeing that it was night time and most patients there were already resting for the evening. It was so quiet. Everything seemed to be low in sound. Once we arrived inside her room, there was a curtain that separated us and her. We slowly entered the room and my heart felt like it dropped into my stomach. I couldn't believe I was in the room with a deceased aunt. To me, I felt as if she was just sleeping. She's been in hospital rooms before. She would be in them for maybe weeks on end. Once she returned home, she would plan a trip to Arkansas where she grew up to visit family who still lived there. While I sat and watched her, I would speak under my breath *in the name of Jesus, wake up auntie!* Repeatedly I would say that hoping that she would just open her eyes and breathe. It never happened. She never rose from her sleep. We all just sat there quietly just watching someone who would never wake up from this. She was gone.

I can only imagine what Jairus and his wife felt. A mother & father who sees the remains of their daughter lying there lifeless. How surreal the experience may have been for them? My grandfather on my mother's side had lost four children prior to his death. Anytime I saw my grandfather lose his children, he was quiet trying to comfort his remaining children. He seemed so at ease, yet calm. I'd never asked him how it felt to lose his children, but I could only wonder what it was like for him. Jesus reminded Jairus to not be afraid, but to only believe. A consolation word from Jesus was all Jairus had - or was it? Jairus asked Jesus upon first meeting Him to come and lay his hands upon his (once living, yet dying) daughter so that she may be healed and shall live. Since then, a woman with a blood issue was healed on the way to Jairus' daughter and now his daughter is dead. Nonetheless, Jesus is still there by way of Jairus' request. Jesus has provided His willingness to go, His display of power, His word of comfort and His ability to discern the unbelievers. The only thing that's left is to perform His ability to honor Jairus' specific request.

The scripture says that Jesus takes the dead girl's hand and says to her *Talitha cumi* which is interpreted *Damsel,* (little girl) *I say unto you, arise* (Mark 5:41 KJV). What? Jesus is talking to a lifeless girl. She's dead. Dead people can't hear, right? On a scientific note, hearing is widely thought to be the last sense to go in the dying process (Blundon et al., 2020). In this context, the girl has already transitioned on. Earlier, Jesus told the weeping crowd that the girl hadn't died at all; she was just sleeping (Mark 5:39). It's possible that Jesus used the word sleep instead of dead euphemistically to challenge the true intent of those who were mourning to determine their real intent of being present at Jairus' house. Jesus wasn't trying to bring comfort to the room. Instead, He set a precedence in place of separating the supporters from the performers. Now that Jesus has set the atmosphere, He can finally honor Jairus' request - lay His hands on her so that she may be healed and shall live.

What's interesting about what Jesus did is that this isn't the way that Jairus wanted things to be done. Jairus wanted Jesus to lay hands on her, not take her by the hand and speak to her dead corpse. I can remember a time when my uncle was looking for housing in a small town in Arkansas. Where he was previously living became less than livable to reside in. The conditions of the residence were beyond repair in regards to his public health and financial ability. Family members were praying on his behalf to receive a better place to live and something very interesting happened. A friend of his had passed away in the process of time, but the place where his friend resided became available for him to move in. When I heard the news, it caught me off - guard. You need to move due to unfit living conditions; you and other family members believe God for a better residence to move into, but a close friend loses their life and you receive the new home for yourself. In one way, you're happy to get the place, but on the other hand someone had to die in order for you to get it. You didn't ask God for them to die to get the house, but you need a better residence for you to live in. Do you not move into the house because it once belonged to a friend? Do you blame God for the loss of your friend? Do you even regret asking God for a better arrangement to reside in? While you ask yourself many questions about what you were believing Him for, the very thing you were believing Him for is still available for the taking. People might even despise you for receiving the blessing due to the circumstances that came along with it. We question so many things and judge others for being involved in the blessing that God had prepared just for you, but should you feel guilty? Should you feel bad about what God has placed in your care to enjoy and be responsible for? Jairus has Jesus by his side. Even in the midst of a mind - boggling journey of faith in Jesus, Jairus has the presence and power of Jesus alongside him. Though Jesus did the exact opposite of what Jairus asked of Him, there doesn't appear to be any issue on the part of Jairus and the dead girl's mother. I believe that the following verse could've been the reason as to why there were no complaints on their part.

In Mark 5:42 (KJV) the bible says that *straightway the damsel arose and walked.* After Jesus speaks to the dead child while taking her hand, immediately she gets up and walks. This twelve-year-old girl got up from her once dead state and everyone in the room was *astonished with a great astonishment.* Their minds are displaced from what has taken place. They're amazed concerning what had just taken place. They've never witnessed anything like this before. It's unbelievable! The key thing to also take away from this is that no one didn't complain as to how Jesus performed this miracle. I think that it's possible to say that many of us have missed God because of how things happened. We seek God to move on our behalf and when He does, we're looking at the process of how things happened. We begin questioning what He did and how He did. We've even asked God why in discontentment because we didn't like the pattern of events that led to the final outcome. All the questioning and emotional baggage that we bring into the moment, yet we overlook the fact that God brought it to pass. Moses has brought the children of Israel near to the place that God has promised them, but because of Moses' disobedience in Numbers chapter 20, he's disqualified from progressing into the Promised Land (Numbers 20:7-12). Nevertheless, the children will still enter the Promised Land with a God - fearing leader in Joshua. 2 Samuel chapter 11 David, who now sits as the king of Israel, has slept with the wife of another man, gets her husband killed and as a result, David will have adversity & violence in his family. Yet, Jesus will be birthed from this lineage as the everlasting King of kings and Lord of lords. You're probably saying what evil happened in Jairus' life that his daughter had to die? None. This wasn't a matter of sin being present. This was about Immanuel manifesting Himself to us. He came to us so that we can come nigh unto Him. Jesus wasn't looking for Jairus, but God sent Jesus so that Jairus could come looking for Him.

Jairus could've used his power, prestige and position to tell Jesus "That's not the way I wanted this to happen!" He could've told Jesus to lay his hands on her like he told Him to. Jairus didn't use his status to make Jesus do anything. It was the posture of the heart that moved Jesus into action. Jesus was moved with compassion despite what Jairus' social & religious status was during that time. Jairus believed Jesus for a miracle. How Jesus ended up doing it was not an issue, especially when the results overpowered the methods. There's a song that says anyway you bless me Jesus, I'll be satisfied. To be able to have a bold conviction in speaking these words, one must be submissive and obedient to the rulership of God. You're saying that your posture will be one of humility. Your mind must be at ease with the methodology of God. Your heart must be soft enough for God's word to penetrate you and rightfully navigate you. Jairus became clay in the hands of Jesus. His faith was molded and shaped. Jairus allowed Jesus to be Jesus to him. His worship was more than just bowing at His feet, but he was acknowledging Jesus by letting Him have control, giving Jesus the authority, space and time to do the miraculous. For Jairus to let Jesus do the miraculous, it took patience, humility, endurance and confidence in Jesus for everything to work out. Jesus had no intention of mishandling Jairus' faith in Him. That's the good news I want to share with you, friend. You didn't partner with Christ for Him to misuse your faith in Him. However, if you're going to seek the miraculous in Him, you must live a life of worship that acknowledges Him. God is giving us the opportunity to trust Him with our all. In turn, you're giving Him the opportunity to prepare the way for you to travel. I remember one time I was on my way to church for Sunday School where I served as a superintendent. As I was on my way to church there was a railroad track coming ahead. As I got closer to the track, the bells rang, the lights flashed and the railing came down. Because I knew the area, I decided to take another route to beat the train and cross on another street, however, by the time I had got there, the rails came down, the bells rang and the railing came down there, too. I called myself beating the train when all I had to do was wait for the train to clear. Because I failed to wait, it took me much longer to get to where I was going when all I had to do was just wait. Many of us don't like the paths we have to take and rather go another way, but sometimes God wants us to stay where we are and stop rushing the process of getting to that place of promise.

If we can be honest with ourselves, we want things to happen for us without difficulty or failure. We don't want any struggle or tough circumstances to interfere with what we want. What we fail to realize is that there are some things that God wants to unveil about us that we didn't know about ourselves. There were some strengths and weaknesses that we didn't know existed. There were gifts and talent that we had no idea was in us. There were even people God had to reveal to us that were with us or against. Had we asked God not to allow these things to happen, imagine where we would be. How would your faith be if you didn't go through the rough patches you experienced? What type of support system would you really have had you not gone through the process? Jairus experienced a sick woman breaking the culture and protocol of the time to receive a faith touch from Jesus. He witnessed people who were around for the show, yet showed no support for him and his wife. He witnessed Jesus exercise His power where people had to clear the atmosphere for Jairus to see who was really there to support him in his time of need. Most importantly, Jairus saw Jesus restore his little girl back to life. I want to encourage you to my fellow brother or sister in the Lord to know that Jesus is still there waiting on you to invite Him where you are and intercede on your behalf. He wants you to trust in His timing, His methods and His message to bring about the miraculous in your life. Even when things appear to go bad, He's still there for you to trust Him to pull you through. If you are someone that has yet to accept Jesus Christ as Lord and Savior, I encourage you to allow this book to be a point of contact to help you understand that God sent Jesus to you so that you can draw closer to Him. You may not understand how God does it, but trust in the fact that He did it with you in mind. We all have had our moments of struggle. Our egos have been humbled and our worlds were rattled. Family was impacted by life's greatest troubles, but you don't have to face these calamities on your own. God has given us the faith to continue on this path called life and no matter where you are in the journey, Jesus is desiring you to allow Him to walk beside you to navigate you to your expected end.

REFERENCES

Blundon, E. G., Gallagher, R. E., & Ward, L. E. (2020, July 8). *Hearing persists at end of life*. ScienceDaily. Retrieved November 19, 2021, from https://www.sciencedaily.com/releases/2020/07/200708105935.htm

Freeman, J. M. (1996). *Manners and Customs of the Bible*. Whitaker House.

Printed in the United States
by Baker & Taylor Publisher Services